FISHING BOATS OF CORNWALL

FISHING BOATS OF CORNWALL

MIKE SMYLIE

The History Press

Barnabas, SS634, 2007, by Roger Lowry.

To Otis Morgan Smylie (born 9/4/09)

First published 2009

The History Press
The Mill, Brimscombe Port
Stroud, Gloucestershire, GL5 2QG
www.thehistorypress.co.uk

Reprinted 2010, 2011

British Library Cataloguing in Publication Data.
A catalogue record for this book is available from the British Library.

ISBN 978 0 7524 4906 7

Typesetting and origination by The History Press
Printed and bound in Great Britain by
Marston Book Services Limited, Didcot

CONTENTS

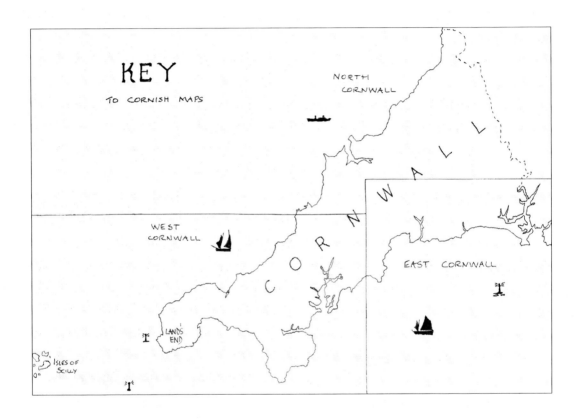

KEY

TO CORNISH MAPS

NORTH CORNWALL

WEST CORNWALL

EAST CORNWALL

LANDS END

ISLES OF SCILLY

CORNWALL

INTRODUCTION

Cornwall is a corner of Britain keen on maintaining a stance marginally apart from the rest of England, slightly mysterious in its shroud of secrecy, yet just as popular for its folklore as for its wonderful coastline and perfect beaches. It is a place of picturesque harbours, dramatic coastal views, jagged rocks with remnants of shipwrecks lying beneath and a history immersed in anarchy. With a coastline extending over 300 miles and a hinterland barely more than ten miles away from the sea or inlet, it is hardly surprising that the sea figures as a vital part of the development of the county and its economy. Trade, fishing and ferrying across river and inlet were the all-important maritime activities, with smuggling, today associated almost exclusively with Cornish hideaways, coming later. First through the novels of nineteenth- and early-twentieth century romantic writers, and later adapted by a desire to attract tourism, Cornwall's smuggling past has perhaps been blown out of proportion, though this illicit 'free-trading', brought about as a countermeasure against the imposition of salt duties on imported salt used in the pilchard industry, did later become a very real and profitable business, extending its arm to tobacco, spirits and luxury goods. Furthermore, the Cornish smugglers leant a hand in the development of faster boats, an influence that rubbed off on its fishing fleets. Richard Carew's survey in the beginning of the seventeenth century confirms the importance of fishing 400 years ago, and he gives a fantastic insight into the various species of fish caught. Fishing for pilchards and mackerel, shoals of which flooded Cornish shores, figured first, until the advent of trawling and later the motorisation of its fleets allowed Cornwall to grow into a major fishing industry. Today Newlyn, right down in the south-west corner of Cornwall, ranks as the port with the largest landings in England, though Devon's Brixham constantly competes with it for this title.

Fishing still plays an important role in many Cornish villages as it has for centuries, though on a much smaller scale due to over-fishing, the European Union's ill thought out Common Fisheries Policy and population movements that have seen locals squeezed out of their traditional villages by wealthy upcountry folk buying up property for use as holiday homes.

What Cornwall has retained, apart from this fishing tradition, is a healthy fleet of traditional fishing craft from the sail and oar era. Many of these are originals from the very late nineteenth and early twentieth centuries, though a number of replicas have also been added to the fleet in recent years. These have primarily been financed by private owners, though a few trusts and associations have, of late, received grants from public bodies for boat restoration, the best example perhaps being the awarding of a Heritage Lottery Grant to the St Ives *Barnabas*, owned by the Cornish Maritime Trust, which is now sailing after a few years languishing in Penryn. At least once a year, at either one of the biennial Looe or Mousehole festivals which are held on alternate years, and of course weather permitting, many of these vessels can be seen sailing in regattas. Competition is fierce at these events, as it was with fishermen of the past. More important than their longevity, perhaps, are the pedigree of boats that have sailed far and wide. In the mid-nineteenth century the Newlyn-built lugger *Mystery* sailed to Australia, a voyage which, at the time of writing, has inspired ocean sailor Pete Goss to build his own lugger, *Spirit of Mystery*, and set sail in her wake. The Looe lugger *Guide Me*, under the ownership of Jono and Judy Brickhill, has sailed across to South America, whilst another Looe boat, *Guiding Star*, has sailed around the Caribbean, crossing the Atlantic for the second time in her history. The Looe-built Polperro gaffer *Vilona May*, restored and skippered by Chris and Marsha Rees, has also sailed the Atlantic, and is rumoured to have sailed to Australia in the 1950s. Though these boats have sailed great distances, in the golden days of fishing under sail Cornish boats sailed up to eastern Scotland yearly to fish for herring, working their way down the North Sea coast following the shoals. Thus, sailing long stretches is nothing new for these craft, and, with the recent upsurge in interest, is set to continue. The following pages, then, are the tip of the iceberg, a brief glimpse into the history and state of these boats today.

We have been pretty lucky over the last hundred years: those with the foresight to catalogue what is a vanishing phenomenon, that of fishing, have done an excellent job. With emphasis today on large technologically perfect fishing boats and ever decreasing fish stocks, fishing is now a job for the lucky few with enough weight to secure huge bank loans, whereas it was once employer to many, who survived without these massive debts.

In the early part of the twentieth century a few members of the Society for Nautical Research, such as H. Oliver Hill and R. Morton Nance, studied Cornish craft, whilst Philip Oke travelled the country drawing the remaining examples. Then came the great Edgar March and his seminal books covering Britain in depth. Cornish boat builders such as Percy Mitchell of Porthmellon and A. S. Oliver of Porthleven have published their memoirs, as have fishermen such as Billy Stevenson of Newlyn and, from Looe, A. J. Pengelly, and, more recently, Paul Greenwood, who fished for many years from Looe and currently owns the 1904-built Mevagissey lugger *Erin*. Robert Simper of Ramsholt has been busy researching and writing about maritime history for over thirty-five years, and sails various beach boats including the newly built Sennen Cove crabber *Silver Stream*. John McWilliams of St Ives, author of two books, whose knowledge of the fishing boats of Newlyn and St Ives is unsurpassed, has aided my work more than anyone through a series of articles in *Fishing Boats*, the thrice-yearly newsletter of the 40+ Fishing Boat Association. For help with photographs I must also thank John, again, and Jan Pentreath of Penpol, both of whom shared their extensive collections with me, the Newquay Old Cornwall Society for their prompt reply to my plea, and Carol Williams who has recently instigated the bringing home of the Porthleven lugger *Provider*. Others with photographs and expertise are, in no particular order: Richard Major, Roger Hosking, Billy Stevenson, John Lambourne, Jim Richards, Martin Castle, Jonny Nance, Fred Saunders, Alan Toms, Heidi Beman, John Buchanan, Nicky Dixon, Martin Ellis, Bryan Roberts, Robert Simper and John Gale. Without the help of any of these, and many more, this book would not have been possible. Thus, this book is more a compilation of what has gone before than a work of primary research, for which I make no excuse.

1

EARLY CORNISH FISHING CRAFT

Percy Robert Craft (1856–1935). *Tucking a School of Pilchards, 1897*. (Penlee House Gallery & Museum, Penzance)

Talk about Cornish fishing and the average person thinks of pilchards, and correctly so, for the Cornish fishing industry has indeed been based upon this small and nutritious fish since time immemorial. I say 'industry' for that was what it was, in the same way that herring created an industry for the Scandinavians, Dutch and eventually Scots, in the North Sea. Massive shoals of pilchards, mature sardines, swamped the Cornish coast in the summer, causing fleets of boats to set out and capture untold numbers of them. For this a heavily framed carvel-built open boat was used, called a *scath ros*, literally a 'net boat'.

Here we immediately see one constructional detail that sets Cornish boats apart from the vast majority of those around the British coasts – the traditional carvel construction – in that the planking of the hull is laid butting up to each other, as against the overlapping clench or clinker tradition of the Scandinavians, or Vikings. Carvel construction is considered to have developed in the Eastern Mediterranean where shell-first carvel construction was used, the planking being adjoined by either wooden pegs or tongue and groove. Shell-first, as it sounds, is a way of boatbuilding where the outer skin is built first and is subsequently strengthened by the addition of internal frames, the way clinker-built vessels are done. However, carvel construction developed a frame-first method, in that the backbone and frames of the vessel were constructed before the outer hull planking was added. Cornish vessels seem to have evolved in a similar fashion to Breton craft, carrying on a tradition that is thought to have travelled north from the Greeks, Venetians and Romans, and later, Iberian traders.

By the early seventeenth century the *cok* seems to have been the typical pilchard boat used in the drift-net fishery, a small open boat with two masts of square-sails, the small foremast being placed well forward in the boat. This is evidenced by several drawings of the time on estate and church maps, all of which show double-ended, bluff-bowed vessels. However, by 1790, we can see an altogether much finer type of vessel being used in which the square sails have been replaced by lugsails, probably influenced by the Breton boats. Indeed, according to Benjamin Ridge, in a lecture he gave in 1893, when referring to Cornish fishing vessels of 1800: 'In rig, size and shape the boats were the very facsimile of those used by the Brittany fishermen of today'. He went on to describe them as 'three-masted luggers, about 34ft keel, and not decked, with a round stern, and possessing sailing qualities superior to any other kind of fishing boat of its size'. By that time the Cornish were seeing the large French Chasse Marée boats, three-masted speedy craft often crewed by the 'pirates and vagabonds' that sometimes came to attack the vulnerable fishing fleets. So impressed were the Cornishmen by these craft that they incorporated three masts into their own craft in the late eighteenth century. Three-masted vessels plied the coast from Land's End right up to the Yorkshire coast, though there were subtle differences in the nature of these fine craft. These craft followed the shoals of herring, pilchards and mackerel, as well as being amongst the first to trawl for fish.

In the drawings of William Daniell made during his circum-navigation of Britain between 1813 and 1823 he shows a number of prints of Cornish harbours and beaches, depicting both gaff-rigged and square-sailed craft. In general the three-masters had done away with the middle mast and become two-masters. In prints of Gorran Haven and Portloe Daniell also shows several double-ended open boats that are, presumably, seine boats of the pilchard fishery, whilst at Penzance similarly-sized beached craft have transom sterns. This seems a bit of a paradox, for it is the East Cornish boats that adopted the transom whilst the West Cornish boats largely retained double-ends in all but their smaller crab boats. Could this picture infer that the Penzance fishermen were the first to adopt the square stern, later to be copied by those from the East? A tenuous claim maybe, but one with a vague possibility of being true! The general consensus is that the transom stern was adopted to give more working space on deck, greater buoyancy aft in the case of smaller crabbers for hauling pots over the after end and, after motorisation, greater buoyancy aft to compensate for the weight of the engine.

THE DEVELOPEMENT OF
THE ST. IVES LUGGER.

Drawings of the development of the Cornish lugger.

By the end of the nineteenth century a pattern does seem to have established itself. Whilst the fishers from Mounts Bay, to the west of the Lizard, used large mackerel drivers (so-called because the fishermen regarded their work as 'driving' the fish into the nets, as against 'drifting' with the nets in tow) and smaller pilchard drivers, all of which were double-ended, those fishing from the east of the Lizard (Falmouth to Looe), as well as Porthleven in Mount's Bay, favoured the transom-sterned lugger. One exception was Polperro where they latterly preferred the gaff rig, as did Plymouth fishermen. Seine-net boats continued to fish pilchards as they had for centuries, whilst a new breed of small crabbing boats began to work off various beaches and tidal harbours.

Penzance, by William Daniell, 1823.

Portloe, by William Daniell, 1823.

2

WEST CORNISH LUGGERS

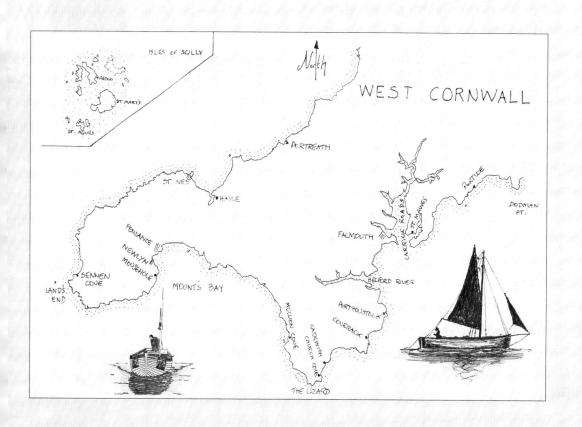

No one knows for sure when the first Cornish lugger as we now know them appeared. It was, in all probability, a gradual metamorphosis with subtle differences being made in hull form from bluff-bowed heavy-sectioned craft to finer, better-designed craft adaptable to the mode of fishing the fishermen were accustomed to. The *Washington Report* of 1849 shows the plans of St Ives and Penzance luggers, both rigged with two masts, though both display a different hull form. Of these two, the St Ives boat is regarded as being generally more advanced in its hull shape, with a sharper entry, finer run aft and a deeper and more upright sternpost. The boat under consideration had been built by William Paynter, one of St Ives' foremost boat builders, and the person responsible for supplying luggers to the Irish Sea and, most notably, the Isle of Man, as well as parts of the east coast of Ireland and the Clyde. What this also illustrates is that

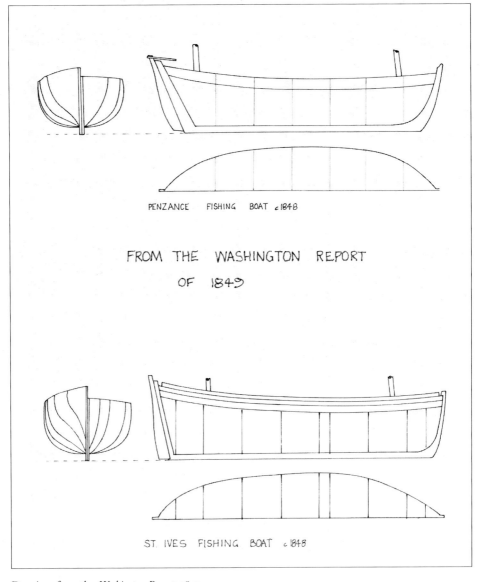

PENZANCE FISHING BOAT c1848

FROM THE WASHINGTON REPORT
OF 1849

ST. IVES FISHING BOAT c1848

Drawings from the *Washington Report*, 1849.

14

there was a fundamental difference between those luggers of Mount's Bay and those based in St Ives. Nevertheless, within twenty years the Mount's Bay boats were overtaking the St Ives boats in terms of hull development.

Fishing boats everywhere evolved through a number of influences brought to bear upon them. Amongst these are the boat builders' and owners' preferences and traditions gleaned through generations of experience, passed down from father to son, then the modes of fishing and the place of shelter from which they had to operate from. The latter is the primary reason for the differences between these two west Cornish types. Though all the harbours – St Ives, Mousehole, Newlyn and Penzance – were tidal, the one at St Ives was more open to the elements. Thus the boats, in adverse sea conditions, had to withstand a heavy pounding as they grounded on the ebb tide. Legs were sometimes adopted, but these usually broke under the constant surges. Boats were therefore fuller-bodied and flatter in the floors to sit upright on the hard sand, and heavier in build to cope with the extra stress. Mount's Bay craft tended to be a bit finer because they were able to sit upon the beach with their legs attached. Both were double-ended in what was a traditional shape, though, in the early years of the twentieth century some were built with transoms, an innovation that spread after motorisation around the end of the first decade of that century. Although one supposition is that they retained the double-ended shape to fit more snugly into overcrowded harbours, this does seem doubtful given that the Cornish had been building double-enders for centuries. Against this is the fact that a few counter and elliptical-sterned boats were later built in both St Ives and Mount's Bay and, towards the end of the nineteenth century, a few transom-sterned boats.

These West Cornish luggers generally came to two sizes. The larger boats, being up to 55ft in overall hull length, were used for the driving of mackerel. Prior to 1830 these craft were open boats while those built after about 1832 had forward half decks and were fully-decked by 1848. They sailed far and wide in search of shoals, joining in with the Irish mackerel fishery off the south coast, drift netting for herring off the east coast of Scotland and England and, again after herring, fishing off the Isle of Man. So impressed were the Manx fishers with these craft that they adopted the design for themselves, referring to the Cornish models as 'nickies'. These boats had accommodation, usually situated aft, for up to seven crew, who could remain at sea for months on end. All were rigged with a dipping lugsail on the foremast and a standing lug on the higher mizzen, sheeted onto a long bumpkin. Sails were high-peaked, and some had mizzen topsails to achieve speeds in excess of ten knots. The design for the higher than normal peaked sails is said to have been imported from Brittany, first adopted by the St Ives men and later taken to Mount's Bay during a regatta in about 1850 when the boat won hands down.

Pilchard drivers were between 20 and 30ft in length. Many tended to be smaller versions of the mackerel drivers in hull shape, though most were half-deckers, with the smallest being open. They set a dipping lug on the mainmast and a smaller standing lug on the mizzen, again sheeted to a bumpkin. They rarely set topsails. Intermediate craft, called 'half- 'n'-halfers', filled the gap between the smaller and large craft, most of which were half-decked and thus only able to fish locally, though these followed the shoals of pilchards, mackerel and herring when in season.

Other than William Paynter, the builders of these exceptionally fine craft include Henry Trevorrow, Robert Bryant and William Williams, all in St Ives, Henry, George and Theodore Peake at Newlyn, another William Williams at Mousehole and Samuel Richards at Penzance. The latter built three boats in Penzance before moving to Lowestoft where he became one of the most notable builders of steam drifters in the early part of the twentieth century.

At Porthleven, on the east side of Mount's Bay, where the original harbour was completed in 1818 (destroyed in 1824 by the sea and rebuilt), the boat building tradition began in about 1850 when Richard Kitto opened up a yard after serving an apprenticeship under Robert Corker Symons of Penzance. The Kittos continued the family tradition up to 1959 when the yard closed, but, in the intervening time, they were responsible for a whole host of luggers destined

Typical fleet of Mount's Bay luggers in light winds. Note the use of sweeps – large oars – to propel the boat, even though the mizzen sail is hoisted.

The harbour at Mousehole with much of the fleet home. The nets are hoisted up the mast to dry after use as constant immersion in salt water rots the cotton fibres. Every month or so the nets are soaked in a solution of stewed oak bark to help preserve them. Catechu, imported from India, was used in the latter days of cotton nets, before man-made fibres superseded them. The crane by the entrance to the harbour was used to drop huge baulks of timber across the entrance when adverse weather was threatening. This crane was removed in the 1970s, though some of the baulks of timber still sit upon the quay today.

Another view of Mousehole, though this time the nets are drying on purposely erected net poles alongside the harbour. These have probably just been barked. Ropes are drying across the boats in the foreground, and these have probably been treated with tar to preserve them.

Mousehole Harbour in about 1880 at low tide with an assortment of luggers and crabbers drying out. The small lugger in the foreground is completely decked-over, except for the large hatch.

Mousehole at low water with boats drying their sails. The smaller pilchard drivers are painted white whilst the large mackerel drivers have dark hulls.

Low water at Mousehole with the harbour packed. Note the difference in size between the two boats alongside each other laid up on the beach.

Mousehole. The two boats in the centre are: PZ602, *Boy Willie*, and PZ634, *Hopeful*, the latter having been broken up in 1927. *Boy Willie* survived into the 1930s when she was measured up by P. J. Oke, whose plans still exist in the Science Museum.

Mousehole on a bright day at high tide. The boat PZ111 is *Veracity* (see Chapter Nine).

Left: Luggers drying out at Mousehole: *Boy Willie*, PZ602; *Renoville*, PZ107; *Nellie Jane*, PZ130; *Muir*, PZ310; *Doreen*, PZ209 and *Boy Don*, PZ459. The man sitting in *Doreen* is believed to be Jimmy Cowls, from the well-known engineers J.T. Cowls & Sons of Porthleven, who fitted many motors, mainly Kelvins, in much of the West Cornish fleet.

Below: Horses and carts awaiting the arrival of the fishing fleet close to the old quay. Once the boats came in, the fish would be loaded into baskets and put aboard the carts bound for Penzance market, or sold locally. Once the railway reached Penzance, fish was sent up country.

Mousehole was a busy fishing harbour in its heyday when it was Cornwall's premier fishing port, though it continued to have a flourishing fleet into the twentieth century. The clinker boat in the foreground is interesting because its construction and shape are reminiscent of boats from the east coast of England.

The motorised transom-sterned lugger *Bonnie Lass* of Mousehole hauling in her drift nets.

A typical West Cornish lugger under full sail, this being *General Havelock*, SS440. Note the long bumpkin used to sheet the mizzen lug. The men are just completing the setting of this sail.

The fleet leaving Newlyn on a calm evening. The peaks of the lugsails are high and, in such calm conditions, the boats tended to drift with the tide rather than sail, until they reached deeper water where they were able to find wind.

The shore at Newlyn in 1882 before the deep-water harbour was built. The beach where the punts are drawn up is now the road with the fish market to the left, whilst the old quay can be seen in the distance.

Another view of Newlyn village taken from its south end in the early 1880s. Note the lugger in the foreground, 50PH, which is clinker-built and registered in Plymouth.

for Cornish owners, as well as down channel as far as Folkestone. Bowdens of Porthleven and the Olivers family were also building from Portleven. The majority of Porthleven luggers were built with a raking transom stern after about 1900 due to the fact that, although the harbour there had existed since 1818, the boats evolved from the smaller beach boats that appear to have been transom-sterned punts. Because of the added deck space other builders adopted transoms, including *Veracity*, PZ111, built in 1902 by J. Blewett of Newlyn and worked from Mousehole. A near replica of this vessel, also called *Veracity*, was launched in 2004.

Mousehole is one of the prettiest harbours along the Cornish coast. It is also famed as having been the first Cornish port to have a breakwater, built in the last decade of the fourteenth century. At the time it was the most important fishing site in Cornwall, which was probably the reason for the harbour's costly construction. This survives today as part of the South Pier, and what remains is the result of improvements made in the eighteenth and nineteenth centuries. Though it was the pilchard that gave rise to the port's importance, this waned in the sixteenth century due to the growth of trade in Penzance, and later Newlyn, but a brief revival in its fortunes came from the mackerel fishery in the mid-nineteenth century when some 430 men fished from there, and another 420 men and women were employed in the shore side activities associated with fishing, such as gutting, packing, curing and coopering. Today it is almost exclusively the domain of pleasure boats, save for one or two potters working crabs and lobsters inshore.

St Ives got its first pier in the fifteenth century, and the outer pier in 1770, though this was extended over a century later, about the same time as the West Pier was added for shipping road stone from the local quarries. Fishing employed both seines and drifting and its pilchard fishery

Newlyn in the 1930s. The counter-sterned lugger *Ocean Pride* is just visible in the bottom left-hand corner of the photograph. This boat still sails (see Chapter Nine).

Newlyn old quay in about 1910, after the deep-water harbour was built. The harbour is full of trading vessels as the the fishing boats tended to continue using the tidal old quay.

Newlyn old quay in 2005. The nearest pier is the Mary Williams Pier, opened in 1980. The North Pier can be seen behind.

The Harbour, St Ives.

St Ives Harbour. The man on the beach to the left is carrying two large fish, possibly having just come ashore from the small punt. Many of the luggers have wheelhouses, which suggests this photo is dated about 1930.

A sea of masts in St Ives Harbour, around the turn of the twentieth century, at high water with all the boats afloat alongside Smeeton's Pier.

HERRING BOATS, ST. IVES

Smaller pilchard drivers setting out. Such boats also drift-netted for herring in the autumn when the pilchard season was over. The mainsail on the nearest lugger is reefed and only one sweep is being used. Each boat carried, on average, five crew, as can be seen in this boat.

Above: Typical St Ives beach scene with many boats dried out. Jousters and carts await loading whilst on-lookers gather. One small girl sits on the beach enjoying the activity.

Left: A close up of several St Ives boats. Note the capstan on the mackerel lugger. The boats inshore are smaller pilchard drivers. The boat on the right is drying her sails.

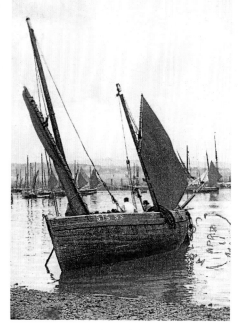

Right: A postcard showing the St Ives pilchard boat *Seven Brothers*, 515SS, built in 1872 and broken up in 1915. It is thought that this picture was taken in the north-east, perhaps North Berwick, and the card was sent from a Leeds address in 1911. For a small 34ft boat to voyage from St Ives to the north-east coast, possibly southern Scotland, was quite a feat, though the voyage to Australia by the lugger *Mystery* shows that much more was possible from these seaworthy craft.

A good view of the deck of the larger mackerel luggers. The boat on the right is registered at St Ives though the sail has a Penzance registration upon it. This was quite usual when sails were lent or bought.

An early twentieth-century view of St Ives. The boat in the centre has legs fitted. This was unusual. The tyres hanging down as fenders suggest the 1920s or 1930s, and the wheelhouses indicate the same period, so these boats were presumably motorised by this time.

Motorised luggers at St Ives. The two in the forefront are *Excellent*, SS122 and *Perseverance*, SS40. The latter was built in 1885 at St Ives and fished for many years under the same ownership as the *Excellent*. Together they were known as 'Percy 'n' Excellent'. The *Perseverance* was sold in 1945 and her name changed to *Moss Rose*.

The *Moss Rose* again after she was sold to Falmouth from St Ives in 1955. At the time she was being used to take out angling parties. This photo came from the cover of a notebook.

Small St Ives pilchard boat *John & Mary*, 467SS, with three crew aboard coming into harbour. The man forward has a sweep ready, perhaps to prevent a collision with the boat on the right sailing out at speed.

The counter-sterned lugger *Iverna*, SS41, after having a motor installed.

An old postcard of Kitto's boatyard at Porthleven in 1912.

Kitto's boatyard from the harbour. The fishermens' nets are simply hanging off the quay to dry. All the luggers at the yard at transom-sterned in the Porthleven style.

The launch of *Provider*, PZ19, in 1955 from the yard of Oliver and Sons, Porthleven. This yard built eighty-seven fishing boats between 1907 and 1961. This boat was the last large fishing boat built at the yard and has more recently been brought back to Porthleven for restoration.

The *Provider* leaving Porthleven in about 1970.

The fleet at Porthleven in the early 1920s. All these boats have transom sterns unlike the vast majority of other Mount's Bay luggers.

was foremost in the whole of Cornwall, being so busy, in fact, that special Acts of Parliament were necessary in 1776 and 1811 to regulate it. This peaked in the 1830s and '40s when some 22 million pilchards were landed yearly. By 1905 there were still 200 fishing vessels registered there, but within a decade seining was over.

Penzance was never a place with a substantial fishery, even if it did gain prominence as an early Mount's Bay fishing harbour in the fifteenth century. The export of tin accounted for the building of its pier in 1766 and plans for the construction of a floating and dry dock in the 1870s coincided with the arrival of the railway which brought holidaymakers destined for the Isles of Scilly, for which it has always been the mainland port of embarkation. Trinity House established a depot there in the 1860s to serve the lighthouses around the Cornish coast and into parts of Devon.

Although its first small quay was built in the fifteenth century, Newlyn was 'a lesser fisher town', according to Richard Carew, in 1602, employed mainly in the taking of pilchards, and it was not until the nineteenth century that this export increased, thus increasing the town's prosperity. Though plans were drawn up for a harbour in 1866, after an initial petition to Parliament was successfully opposed by Penzance, work was stalled until a great storm in 1880 wrecked some thirty boats in Mount's Bay, including nine in Newlyn and one, the Mousehole lugger *Jane*, as it attempted to enter Penzance. Horrified onlookers watched the small vessel being smashed to pieces and the crew drowned. Work on the artificial harbour started within years, and was completed by 1894. Newlyn now had a harbour accessible in all states of tide. Its fishery expanded at the expense of smaller beach-based communities. Today it remains the premier port in Cornwall, and jostles with Brixham as the principal port in England. Only the major Scottish ports of Peterhead, Fraserburgh and Lochinver can boast substantially higher landings.

The fishing registration letters for St Ives are SS, whilst the majority of Mount's Bay vessels are registered at Penzance with the letters PZ, though this was, at one time, PE.

The counter-sterned driver/long-liner *Rosebud*, PZ87, in front of the Houses of Parliament in 1937. She had been built in 1919 by Joseph Peake & Sons of Newlyn. When the local council was planning to demolish several streets of fishermen's housing in Newlyn there was uproar. They had been declared 'slums' by the council, yet the inhabitants regarded this as an act mirroring the Scottish clearances. In a final bid of desperation to prevent the destruction of their homes and the building of blocks of flats, the fishermen sailed this boat to London with a petition from the local population. The nation was captivated by reports in the press and film newsreels. Though the inhabitants received a reprieve, some housing was still knocked down, though not on the scale originally planned.

Another view of *Rosebud* in Newlyn. She fished from Newlyn for many years until being sold to a consortium trying to locate the *Titanic*. The project failed and the boat ended up on the saltings at Lelant where so many Mount's Bay luggers ended up. She was eventually pulled up into a car park and locals were invited to come and take away souvenirs. Many a model boat exists in Penwith made with timber from the old boat.

3

EAST CORNISH LUGGERS

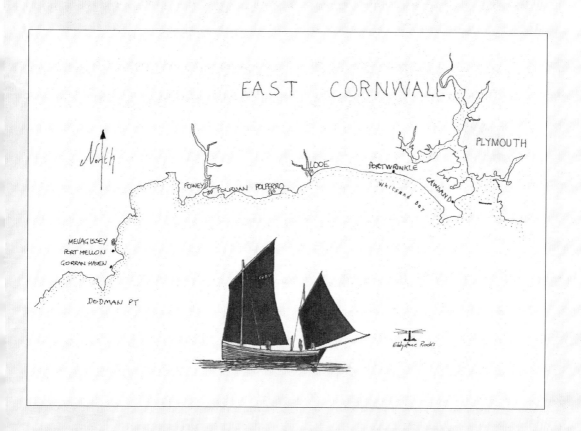

The principal fishing harbours east of the Lizard were Mevagissey, Looe and Polperro, and each had its own fleet of transom-sterned luggers, though there were small fleets based in sheltered facilities at Falmouth, Gorran Haven and Fowey. Furthermore, we have already seen how Porthleven fishing boats were generally transom-sterned. Why, then, this fundamental difference between the double-ended boats to the west and these transom-sterned craft of the east?

The answer must surely lie in the fact that these eastern harbours were more sheltered then those of St Ives and Mount's Bay. But even that doesn't explain why they adapted their earlier boats with transom sterns, assuming that these earlier boats were double-ended. The transom is generally regarded as being adopted from the small transom-sterned beach boats that worked all along the south coast of England and further afield. Although more sheltered, the three main harbours still dried out at low water, and thus the boats had to take to the ground with legs fitted to keep them upright. What does seem to be the case is that these fishers adapted to change, whereas those of Mount's Bay kept to tradition. Did that alone account for their adoption of the transom-sterned vessel?

According to H. Oliver Hill the luggers from the east were, in the mid-nineteenth century, small open boats, and it was from these that the larger half-decked boats evolved later in the century. What is telling is that, between 1860 and 1870, Mevagissey built some half dozen large-decked, counter-sterned boats, the biggest of which was 45ft in the keel and 55ft overall. These were not deemed a success and were eventually sold on to the east coast of England. This, then, leads to the conviction that the larger-decked boats, like the Mount's Bay craft, were not suited to the ways of fishing from these ports.

The first Mevagissey lugger to sail to the North Sea was the 32ft *Band of Hope* in 1863. All she had was a 9ft-long cuddy and four men, and occasionally a boy, lodged within this confined space. Whereas that scale of accommodation might have been perfectly normal for inshore fishing close to home, for exceptionally long voyages hundreds of miles away from home it must have been pretty uncomfortable for those involved. Ten years later, when the *Rival* followed the same route, things had only improved slightly with 9in waterways and a low deck in the stern sheets at the after end of the boat. However, this had begun the trend to improve seaworthiness, and before long these luggers were all being decked, though their size hardly increased. The accommodation still remained at the forward end in what was originally the cuddy, with the decked space aft being used for net stowage, sails and other gear. The average size of these craft was 33ft in the keel and almost 40ft in overall length. Only in one or two of the decked vessels of the period 1870–80 was the crew's accommodation aft.

These luggers, like their western counterparts, were rigged with a dipping mainsail and standing lug mizzen, though they seldom, if at all, set a mizzen topsail. Again, unlike the western luggers, they usually set a jib on a running bowsprit when making passage, some even setting a mizzen staysail. They generally drift-netted for pilchards, mackerel and herring, working long-lines at other times. As to the differences between Looe and Mevagissey boats: there were hardly any except that the Mevagissey boats had a slightly more raking stern.

The shape of the Mevagissey tosher was the same as the lugger, though a lot smaller at less than 20ft in length, as is generally thought, to avoid the payment of harbour dues. These small open boats, rigged with one gaff sail, were used for inshore long-lining and hand-lining for mackerel.

Several boat builders worked in Looe including Peter Ferris, Dick Pearce, Jas Angear and Arthur Collins, whilst at Mevagissey the principal builders were Frazier Bros and Henry Roberts (senior and junior). Percy Mitchell set up business in Porthmellon, a mile west of Mevagissey, in 1925, after completing his apprenticeship with Henry Roberts junior in his yard which was in a disused pilchard curing store in the middle of Mevagissey. Robert senior had previously been based in Porthmellon but moved back to Mevagissey when the new road was built. How long a boatyard had been there is unknown, though a Mr Dunn was building vessels there in the early

1800s. Percy Mitchell became one of the best known of the Cornish boat builders, working there until his retirement in the late 1960s. Described as 'an artist in wood' and as 'one of the finest traditional boatbuilders in the world', he produced some of the best Cornish fishing boats ever made, even after motorisation had taken hold of the fleets. Porthleven, as we have seen, has built many of the east Cornish luggers which, in contrast to the general yacht-like lightness of the Mevagissey and Looe boats, were often regarded as being 'rough as rats, but strong and sturdy', a reference to their heavier build. Another famous Cornish boat builder, Richard (Dick) Pill, worked from nearby Gorran Haven building both luggers and crab boats until his death in 1926. Today, one of the only traditional boat builders still working along the Cornish coast is John Moor, based in a corner of Frazier's old yard where he has been since 1976. He was first apprenticed to Percy Mitchell and, though responsible for a multitude of fishing boats, sees little business in that direction today.

Polperro was the exception for although it did have its own fleet of luggers their existence was short-lived. Before the late nineteenth century fishermen preferred to rig their boats with spritsails. Up to about 1860 these craft had been clinker-built, thus showing influences from further east along the channel to Plymouth, with its Royal Navy associations, where clinker construction and the sprit were more common. At about 30ft in length, they also set a foresail, and in some cases a topsail and small mizzen. Due to severe weather, in 1891, when most of the fleet of a dozen vessels or so had been wrecked, the fishermen turned to gaff-rigged carvel boats to replace their craft, many of these coming from Looe and Mevagissey boat builders. Rigged with a boomless main and topsail, these boats were about 25ft in length and became known as the Polperro Gaffers. Further along the coast, at Cawsand and Kingsland, within Plymouth Sound, similarly rigged Plymouth hookers worked.

Mevagissey's first stone pier dates from 1430 and was lengthened in 1776 with another pier being added on the western side. By about 1850 there were eighty fishing vessels working from the port supporting more than 300 fishermen and others working in associated trades. The port persisted as an important fishing harbour with a thriving fleet until the late twentieth century, and although a few boats are still based there, pleasure yachts outnumber these by at least ten to one. Most of the boats still fishing land in nearby Looe.

Looe is today Cornwall's number two fishing port and boasts a modern electronic auction system in its fish market alongside the quay, from where fish are sent all over Western Europe. The town is split into east and west by the river of the same name, and it is solely because of this that Looe exists as a port. It used to be one of the busiest harbours in the south-west until Fowey and Plymouth surpassed it, though it experienced a brief renaissance in the nineteenth century with exports from the rich mines above Liskeard. The fishing fleet, though, has been well established and today is keeping alive a harbour that is otherwise patronised by the holidaymakers that throng to Looe in season.

Polperro has been described as a place best entered by sea, for it seems that the harbour is a mere fault in the rocks. Once in and around the small breakwater, the harbour is little more than a creek surrounded by quaint buildings and hillside. It is probably the best known of Cornish villages and in summer is filled to bursting point with visitors. Sadly it has become a sort of shrine to tourism that seems to spill out of every doorway with advertisements, ice-cream parlours and the like. It has been a fishing community since at least 1303, and has continued into the twentieth century. It has also been the haunt of smugglers, now grossly over-exaggerated, and home to artists and writers and other famous folk. Today there is not much fishing remaining for, as in Mevagissey, Looe took away its trade. Of the boats that decorate the harbour most are for pleasure or charter whilst a few work inshore grounds for mackerel and crabs.

Fishing boats along this coast display either FH (Falmouth) or FY (Fowey) registration letters, though several PH (Plymouth) boats may be seen. Others using the letters TO are registered in Truro.

West wharf, Mevagissey, not long after 1918. A boat alongside is loading barrels whilst a few fishing boats are in the harbour. A couple have been painted bright colours, a tendency from this time onwards.

Opposite above: A view looking over Mevagissey Harbour. Some eighty fishing boats worked out of this harbour in the late nineteenth century. A couple of toshers can be seen in the forefront.

Opposite below: Mevagissey Harbour in about the 1880s. It was not until the 1880s that the fishing boat registration system altered so that the numbers came after the port letters.

The lugger *Ibis* having her bottom scrubbed and repainted at Mevagissey. The boat is deep at the fore end and there is a propeller aperture in the stern that dates this photo to the 1920s/'30s.

Mevagissey in 1909. *Ella*, FY4, is a tosher, whilst the harbour seems quite full of larger luggers drying their sails.

1909, again with one boat hauled up and dried out for ongoing repairs and scrubbing. She's gaff-rigged and half-decked which suggests she's a Polperro gaffer. Why is the little boy slapping the hull!?

Toshers in Mevagissey. These boats were mostly less than 20ft in length to escape payments of harbour dues.

The work of baiting long-lines continued long after the boats had returned in readiness for the next trip out.

Left: View of a gaff-rigged vessel *Sea Wave*, 158FY, alongside and dried out at Fowey. Note the very sharp forefoot and the tall topmast.

Below: Several luggers moored alongside the west quay in Looe. The middle boat is *Guiding Star*, FY363, whilst the boat moored alongside is *Guide Me*, FY233. Both these boats remain sailing today.

The lugger *Our Daddy*, FY7, built by Dick Pierce of Looe in 1921, alongside Looe East Quay.

Looe East Quay. The lugger *Our Boys*, FY221, has landed whilst the smaller lugger is coming alongside. *Our Boys* was another built by Dick Pierce in 1904.

Our Boys again in the 1960s at Looe.

The fish market on the East Quay at Looe with fish being unloaded. Note the 'iron man' capstans sitting on the quay, probably redundant as a new wave of winches were fitted into the boats.

Two clinker-built boats that have been damaged at Polperro. It is presumed that these are two of the older luggers that were damaged in the storm of 1891, after which they adopted what became known as the Polperro gaffer.

The harbour at Polperro, seen here in about 1890, nestles in a gap in the cliffs. It is protected by two small inner piers that date back several centuries, although they have been severely damaged and repaired over the years, as have the fleets of boats within the harbour. The outer pier was not built until the 1860s. The harbour could be closed off in the event of a storm. The crane lowered the baulks of timber that can be seen with drying nets laid over them, which the fishermen also dried by hanging over the pier.

Above: The Polperro gaffer *Lady Beatrice*, FY 384, leaving Polperro. Most of these vessels were built in Looe.

Right: The fleet leaves Polperro in calm seas. Here the *Two Sisters* is seen under sail. This boat is entirely open and has four men aboard, though the man standing by the helmsman appears to be too well dressed to be a fisherman. Maybe he's along for the ride!

Left: Polperro Harbour in about 1910. The boats are half-deckers, and *Lady Beatrice* can be seen again in the middle. The sculling punt has a can of what appears to be petrol or paraffin, suggesting that at least one boat had an engine.

Below: The dried out harbour of Polperro with many gaffers in. These boats were mainly used for long lining, though they did fish for pilchards and herring during the season. The houses in Polperro reach right into the harbour and have helped to give the place a mysterious feel, encouraged by stories of smuggling. Today it is a haven for tourists who crowd its narrow streets.

4

CRAB BOATS AND BEACH LANDINGS ON THE SOUTH COAST

The small harbour of Portwrinkle on Cornwall's 'forgotten coast' was once home to a thriving, if small, fleet of inshore potting boats. Today only a couple of pleasure boats can be seen here, and only then if you are lucky.

I think that, in terms of active research in the field, beach landings are far more interesting and exciting than those done in artificial harbours. Much of this is to do with their inaccessibility and the often beautiful surroundings of what were once the tiny and remote haunts of fishermen and smugglers. Visiting some of these around the Cornish coast involves a hike along a stretch of coastal footpath, whilst others lie several miles at the end of very narrow and windy lanes. In a recent day's traipsing around I visited the tiny beach under the lee of Pendeen Head, another equally small beach at Porthgwarra and the slightly larger Penberth Cove: three absolutely delightful but steep beach landings, though only the latter has any semblance of fishing today. Here, too, is a fully restored capstan winch, once so common upon many of these beach landings, now, sadly, the last remaining example. Most of these landings were born upon the pilchard, but as those shoals deserted them, the locals turned to potting instead.

The term 'crab boat fishing' generally also refers to lobster and crayfish fishing using pots, all three of which were prolific along the rugged Cornish coast. Most operated from the small tidal harbours and beach-based landings that dot the coastline. Generally the craft were under 20ft in overall length, though some of those in use at Sennen Cove were marginally bigger. These boats were a compromise between speed and carrying capacity, especially when loaded with the Cornish withy pots sometimes referred to as 'inkwell' pots. The boats were all transom-sterned with a full body and relatively fine entry at the bow. They also tended to be strongly built for the type of work they undertook, working directly off beaches. They worked in large numbers and there was hardly any accessible cove that didn't have one single boat at the very least. Today they have largely disappeared, replaced by modern craft, though a few living examples such as the Cadgwith crabber *Minerva* still exist. Gorran Haven has one or two still working part-time, whilst replicas of the Sennen Cove crabbers have been built recently at the Falmouth marine school.

Opposite page: Polkerris, once home to several pilchard seines and, in the twentieth century, home to a fleet of crabbers.

Crabbers at Gorran Haven. These boats have engines yet many retained a small mizzen steadying sail until the 1930s. Here, seen in the 1950s, only one boat still has a mizzen.

Two crabbers at Gorran Haven in about 1998. These are only used in the summer season. During a recent trip to Gorran Haven in mid-November there were no boats to be seen in the harbour.

The 17ft Gorran Haven crabber sailing at the Newlyn Fish Festival, August 2008. Owned by the Cornish Maritime Trust, she was built in 1882 by Dick Pill of Gorran Haven, and was reputed to be the fastest afloat. She was, like many of the Gorran Haven crabbers, sprit-rigged. By 1900, because the harbour there was becoming too crowded, she moved to Flushing. She was eventually restored in the 1990s and bought by the trust for £1.

Around Veryan Bay the small village of Portloe had its own fleet of crabbers. Here, in 1626, there were eight fishermen in the village. Most of these boats are clinker-built, which was unusual for Cornish boats and probably reflected the skills of a single boat builder, probably local. Most of these small boats have engines fitted and the photo was probably taken in the early 1950s.

Portloe in 2003. The beach is steep and the photo here shows modern crabbers drawn up the slipway. The wooden boat in the centre of the photo is similar in shape to the old sailing boats though she is more full-bodied because of the added weight of the engine, and to carry more pots. This boat was probably built by John Moor in Mevagissey.

In the next bay west of Portloe, Gerrans Bay, lies the harbour of Portscatho which has latterly relied upon the crab and lobster summer fishing. However, it had previously been pilchard seining that occupied the fishermen's calendar. At the beginning of the eighteenth century there were eleven pilchard cellars in the village. However, fishing was not at that time the principle source of employment for, due to the proximity of the village to Falmouth, most men went to sea on the Falmouth packets or merchant vessels, and worked on site. It was the older men who fished in Gerran's Bay: in the mid-century, the vast majority were over sixty years of age.

Antoinette, FH626, a small wooden motorised crabber on the beach at Porthoustock in about 1998. Porthoustock is a fishing cove that became dominated by jetties used to load road stone onto ships from nearby quarries. By the 1960s the beach was once again solely occupied by fishermen though their numbers can, today, be counted on one hand.

Compared to Porthoustock, Coverack had a substantial harbour that was capable of holding trading vessels as well as having its own fleet of crabbers. The largest boat, in the centre of the photo, still has its mizzen sail, though most had been converted to motor power by the time this photo was taken.

The beach at Cadgwith with crabbers drawn up and pilchard seiners higher up. It is said that Cadgwith thrived on smuggling, pilchards and crabs, though today tourism is its highest earner.

A postcard of two crabbers (on the right) in the 1950s. Open boats of about 19ft, these were painted in light colours in the twentieth century and fitted with engines after about 1930.

A postcard sent in 1962 from J.W. while on holiday in Cadgwith – 'getting around a bit', according to the card's text. Eight crabbers are lined up on the beach, brightly painted. They retain their mizzenmasts and sails to steady the boats whilst at sea, especially when working their pots.

What is believed to be a Cadgwith crabber on the beach. Again, this is unusual because it is clinker-built.

A typical Cadgwith crabber. *Minerva*, FH58, was built in the village in 1935. Though having an engine fitted, she is still rigged with a mizzen sail with a bumpkin, the hole for which can be seen in the transom. Engine reliability was poor until after the Second World War. This boat has recently been bought and hopefully will soon be restored.

Church Cove, a short distance from Cadgwith, had its own fleet that was hauled up the steep landing by capstan.

The Lizard, Church Cove.

Around the Lizard lies Mullion Cove, shown here in about the 1880s before the pier was built in the next decade. These boats, similar to those from Cadgwith, were rigged with two lugsails, the foresail a dipping lug whilst the mizzen was a standing lug. Winches such as the one shown here were commonplace on beaches such as this.

MULLION · COVE.

Above: Penberth (2008) still with colourful boats drawn up and the winch was has been restored by the National Trust.

Right: Colourful boats at Penberth.

Opposite above: Mullion Cove after the harbour was built. Two larger crabbers sit on the beach with their bumpkins set. Today the harbour is owned by the National Trust, and rumour has it that they are not going to repair the harbour wall again, presumably due to the cost and the fact that few boats use it. It remains at the mercy of winter storms.

Opposite below: Penberth Cove, home to a thriving fleet of crabbers for centuries. The winch atop the beach is typical of many found in these small Cornish beach landings.

Porthgwarra, a few miles west of Penberth, is another steep beach landing that, nevertheless, had a vibrant small fleet of crabbers.

View of the Porthgwarra boats in the late 1930s. The boats on the left are small punts that never went far out to sea, whilst the larger boat on the right went crabbing. Like the Lizard boats, these were deeper in section than those from further east.

The harbour at Sennen Cove, Land's End, must be one of the most exposed in Britain. Nevertheless, fishermen set their pots all around this rocky and wild coast. The size of the small boats are formidable given the position of the harbour and the waters they worked in.

Sennen Cove, Land's End, with two crabbers on the right and a seiner on the left. The famous *Round House* houses the capstan used to haul the boats up. This was built in 1876, and the capstan came from a redundant tin mine. Today it houses an art gallery.

A typical Sennen Cove small pilchard driver that probably doubled as a crabber. The bumpkin for the mizzen sail is almost as long as the boat itself.

Lines and construction plans exist for those crabbers from Cadgwith, Gorran Haven, Porthgwarra and Sennen Cove, so we can understand the shapes which enabled these replicas to be built. Similar craft worked from villages such as Portloe, Portscatho, Coverack, Mullion Cove and Penberth, the latter having had its beach winch restored by the National Trust. Crabbers also worked out of the larger ports mentioned in the last chapter such as Polperro, Mevagissey and Newlyn, as they still do today. To the north, as we shall see in a subsequent chapter, the coast is much more rugged and hostile, resulting in far fewer fishing harbours and beach communities and much less fishing. This part of the coast is also much more open to the vagaries of the Atlantic weather systems.

The rigs of these crab boats tended to mirror the larger luggers with big dipping lug mainsails and smaller standing lug mizzens. As often as not, though, because the fishing grounds were close to home and the pots had to be lifted and re-baited each day, the boats were rowed by a three-man crew. Regional differences in the boats were small: some had centreboards to increase stability whilst the larger and older Sennen Cove boats had washboards with shuttered cut-outs for the oars, presumably because of the openness of their fishing grounds around Land's End. Most crabbers were carvel-built though a few clinker examples once worked these shores.

Fibreglass crab boats on the slip at Sennen Cove in 2002. Note the winches and outboard engines. These boats are fairly standardised throughout Cornwall now.

Making withy pots at the Newlyn Fish Festival in 2008.

A Cornish fisherman with his withy lobster pots. These are of the standard Cornish design and today several folk build them in the same way, though the majority of fishermen now use steel framed pots.

5

MISCELLANEOUS FISHING CRAFT

The clinker-built St Ives gig *Four Brothers*, SS165, with the boom being used as a hoist by the boat behind.

ST IVES GIG

Following the autumnal herring season from St Ives, many fishermen utilised a smaller version of the pilchard driver. Clinker-built rowing and sailing gigs, heavier than the pilot gigs and measuring between 26 and 32ft, were either rowed by four oars or sailed with a dipping lug mainsail and a small standing lug or sprit mizzen. Some had centreboards enabling them to sail faster, and most were built in St Ives, though a few worked out of Newquay to the north. Their main asset was being able to get to sea whilst the heavier boats were still ebbed by the tide, thus enabling the fishermen a quick shot or two in advance of the bigger boats. With the onset of motorisation in the 1910s, gigs increased in length up to 40ft, but they retained their openness although the engine, or engines, had a cambered cover over. Tommy Thomas was a prolific builder of these craft in St Ives, working from his boatshed on the promenade, as was Henry Trevorrow and a fellow called Landers. One or two double-ended seine boats were converted into gigs by having a transom stern built on. Some forty carvel motor gigs were built in total in St Ives, mostly in the 1920s. Whereas Newlyn built motor pilchard drivers, St Ives built motor gigs that were capable of carrying large amounts of herring. They kept the mizzen lugsail for lying to their drift nets. By the end of the 1920s these gigs had developed with wheelhouses being fitted, short foredecks added and a higher freeboard. Most were painted light blue whereas the sailing gigs were white. By the 1940s they were hardly recognisable, with capstans fitted for crabbing and trawling. Few remain, though St Ives still has two working as canopy launches, whilst *Caronia*, SS70, a rare gig built in 1927 by Peakes of Newlyn, now called *Starfish*, has become a pleasure yacht.

It must also be remembered that gig fishing was not just confined to St Ives, and that gigs from other beaches and harbours were used for inshore fishing as well, especially hand-lining, while others were at one time used for mullet seining. These fishing gigs, however, should not be confused with the pilot gigs which today are numerous, having undergone a renaissance in the last decade or two, with weekly rowing regattas during the summer and an annual international championship in the Scilly Isles. Moreover, questions have been asked as to why gig racing is not an Olympic sport! Indeed, why not?

ST IVES JUMBO

In the 1880s, some St Ives fishermen were not keen on gigs, perhaps due to the fact that many were wrecked, and when they wanted a smaller vessel than the pilchard driver they opted for what became the 'Jumbo' – a vessel unique to the town. The name is perhaps misleading, for 'jumbo-ising' referred to the habit of lengthening boats, something that some Cornish owners opted for in the 1920s when new boats cost too much and there was a dearth of older boats. Boats such as *Pioneer*, PZ277, *Ripple*, SS19, and *Rosalind* (ex-*Susan*, SS185), all of which are still sailing, the latter in the USA, are examples of this trend. Jumbos in St Ives were, it is said, named after an African elephant in London Zoo, the most popular attraction, which was sold to the USA in 1882 causing a national outcry.

In St Ives, though, a Jumbo was a baby version of the pilchard driver, a small double-ended clinker or carvel boat, totally open, crewed by some three fishermen and rigged with two lugsails in a similar fashion to the pilchard boats. Length was about 24 to 29ft, and those below 25ft were clinker, whilst larger craft tended to be carvel built. According to the late Eddie Murt, who spent a lifetime researching St Ives fishing boats, there were about twenty-plus Jumbos in the 1880s, two of which were probably converted ships' lifeboats. Small in number, they were also short-lived, often referred to as 'old men's boats' and were not generally favoured. William Paynter of St Ives certainly built one or two: a copy of his draft has survived, now in the National

Maritime Museum, from the 1880s. Paynter describes these boats as being built 'for John Uren & others'. Boat builder Jonny Nance, also of St Ives, has recently built a small clinker replica of these craft, *Celeste*, the first to sail in the bay for many years, and he hopes to build more so that these Jumbos can race together once again.

FALMOUTH WORKING BOAT

The waters of the River Fal and around the Carrick Roads are home to a unique oyster fishery that for over 500 years has been fished by sailing boats or under oar, and continues to do so in the same manner due to a local by-law of 1876 and certain EU restrictions. In the shallow water small punts are used to drag a dredge across the beds, but in the deeper water the Falmouth Working Boat is used. On average these craft are 23ft in length, though some are larger, up to 30ft in fact. They are all gaff-rigged, transom-sterned and carvel built, many with a cuddy under the foredeck. Many were built locally specifically for the job, though others have been imported from around Britain, making the fleet one of the most diverse of the sailing era. One boat, *Zigeuner*, FH89, was famously built in Germany, then rebuilt in Restronguet in the 1840s, and fished up to the 1940s. The fishery still survives, just, though pollution, stress of the job, retirement amongst the older fishers and unwillingness amongst newcomers to persevere, has depleted the number of boats working the dredges to a mere handful.

Fibreglass versions of these craft have been built at Martin Heard's boatyard in Mylor Creek, and many of these, with their heightened rigs, race out of St Mawes during the summer months when there's no oyster dredging to be done. When working, Falmouth Working Boats carry about 300-square-feet of sail, but when racing this increases to the voluntary limit of a massive 1,000-square-feet. Most have no engines and are very handy boats to race.

SCILLONIAN PILOT CUTTER

Scillonian pilot cutters once plied the Western Approaches in their search for incoming ships, to offer them pilotage into various British ports, including Liverpool. They were hardy vessels, going out in all weather with up to seven pilots aboard. When not piloting, they were often as not carrying cargo out to vessels or even around the Scilly Isles where they were built, shipbuilding being a thriving industry there in the days of wooden sailing craft. Some of these pilot cutters, it has been suggested, even fished when things were quiet. Today there are none left. Their era was from the late eighteenth century to the 1880s, though several replica boats have been built by Working Sail of Gweek. The last surviving pilot cutter was the *Agnes*, built in 1841 and cut up in Tresco to be used as fencing posts in 1902.

St Ives in the herring season. The gig *Glorious Peace* is on the left, with two clinker-built gigs in the foreground and a pilchard boat on the right.

Building a gig on the beach at St Ives in the 1920s, in what was probably Henry Trevorrow's yard.

Three motorised gigs amongst the fleet at St Ives in the 1920s. These (in the foreground) are: *Highflyer*, *Garfield*, SS151 and *Little Johnnie*, SS128. Many St Ives reservists were serving upon HMS *Highflyer* when it sank the German auxiliary cruiser *Kaiser Wilhelm der Grosse*, hence the name of the gig.

St Ives before the west pier was built in 1894. Two pilchard boats are identifiable: *Annie*, SS34, and *Helena Maud*, SS537. The five boats in the foreground are all Jumbos: two clinkers and three carvel.

A gaff-rigged St Ives Jumbo with a beam trawl hanging from the mast to dry.

Celeste at her moorings in St Ives Harbour in 2008.

The St Ives Jumbo *Annie Beatrice*, SS84, under full sail in calm seas.

The new Jumbo *Celeste* in 2007. She is 20ft and 6in in length and clinker built.

The Falmouth working boat *George Glasson* drifting sideways down the tide over the Carrick Roads oyster beds in 1974. She was built in 1898 in Porthleven as a lug-rigged pilchard driver and was half-decked. She started oyster dredging in 1923, at which time she was converted to a gaff cutter, a rig much more suited to dredging.

The *George Glasson* at Mousehole, 2006, after being restored with a more powerful rig for racing.

Another Falmouth working boat preparing for a race at St Mawes, 2008.

The Falmouth working boat *Softwing*, now belonging to the Cornish Maritime Trust.

Scillonian pilot cutters *Atlantic* (built 1841) and *Presto* (built 1860) on the beach at St Agnes in the late nineteenth century.

The Scillonian replica pilot cutter *Agnes*, built in 2003 by Luke Powell of Working Sail in Gweek, sailing off Brittany in 2008. The original *Agnes* was built in 1841.

6

THE NORTH COAST

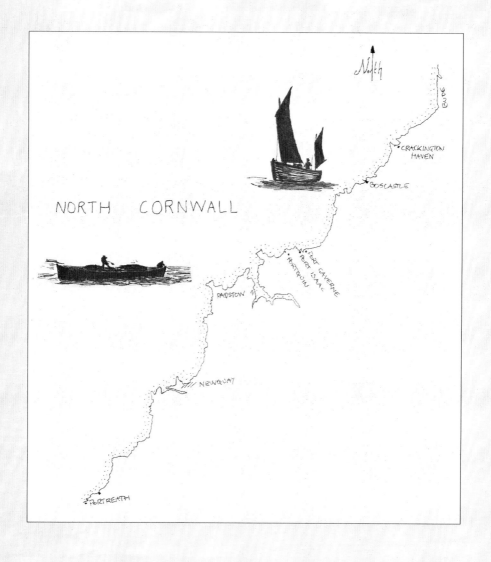

North

BUDE

CRACKINGTON
HAVEN

BOSCASTLE

NORTH CORNWALL

PORT GAVERNE

PORT ISAAC

PORTQUIN

PADSTOW

NEWQUAY

PORTREATH

The north Cornish coast is one of the most inhospitable in England: along with some of the highest cliffs, it has few artificial harbours and protected coves. Thus, in comparison to the south coast, with the exception of St Ives, this coast has attracted little research, apart from John Bartlett's formidable *Ships of North Cornwall*. The few harbours it does have are either sheltered from the Atlantic seas that the coast faces by headlands or nestled in river estuaries and narrow coves. Of these, again with the exception of St Ives which we have already discussed, Padstow and Newquay are perhaps the oldest since they have had quays dating back many centuries. Portreath, up the coast from St Ives, has extensive harbour workings that date from the mid-eighteenth century and were constructed to harness trade from the nearby mines over in South Wales. Fishing, though, had long been in existence from this cove, and continued after the harbour was first built and the inner basin added in the mid-nineteenth century. The entrance is famed for being the most difficult of those on the north coast to enter from the sea, though that in no way infers that the others are easy!

There was once a small harbour at St Agnes, though the sea has long since destroyed it. In fact, there were five attempts at building piers between 1632 and 1920, when the last one was washed away, and it is hard to believe today that schooners were once built here. Perranporth, now the domain of surfers, once supported several seine companies whose seine boats were kept under the lee of the cliffs on the beach. Likewise, Newquay is now a place dedicated to surfing, though the first pier was built there in the early fifteenth century. The 'new quay' was built as a harbour of refuge rather than for import or export trades, for only a tiny hamlet existed there at the time. Pilchard companies saw an opening and Newquay, as it soon became known, supported many companies and their curing cellars. The harbour was built in 1833 and subsequently sold for development as an export of china clay. Facilities were improved in the 1870s, yet by the 1920s trade was declining. The central quay, which today appears as an island, was once connected by a wooden structure over which locomotives would chug pulling trucks loaded with china clay. However, this same railway soon carried passengers at about the time the harbour expanded in 1870 and, with boarding houses being erected, tourism arrived. Today it is this same tourism that sustains the local economy. Some fishing boats work out of the harbour today, mostly potting.

The tiny coves along this coast were home to several pilchard companies, but were also the haunts of smugglers. Some have suggested that smugglers built the steps in the rocks at Bedruthan Steps, a long sandy beach with dramatic stacks of rock along its fringe. Not a good place to base pilchard seines, but a possibility all the same! Padstow, around Trevose Head, is situated on the west bank of the estuary of River Camel with its notorious 'Doom Bar' entrance, and is as renowned today for being the home of Rick Stein's seafood restaurant as anything else – a sure sign of its maritime decline! As the largest, and probably oldest, port on the north coast, trade was principally the export of slate, tin and copper, with goods such as coal, limestone and timber coming in for the local inhabitants. Though its first pier is younger than Newquay's, dating from the sixteenth century, it seems certain that boats were drawn up here on the muddy beach, back in the days of the Domesday book. However, it was not until the end of the eighteenth century that serious harbour-building programmes began, encouraged by a healthy shipbuilding business. Padstow also became a customs base, set up to counter smuggling. Herring was landed here in the early days of the twentieth century, much of it by boats from eastern England, to be taken by the new railway to Billingsgate. Padstow was joined to the national rail network in 1899. Today the town maintains a small fishing fleet of a varied types, whilst the inner harbour is now a floating harbour for yachts.

The three ports, Portquin, Port Isaac and Port Gaverne, have to be amongst the most lovely and genuine coastal villages in Cornwall. Over time they have been home to small fleets of mostly small crabbing and inshore boats. These boats have tended to reflect those from the south coast, though a few larger luggers did work from here. Portquin had its own pilchard cellars and fleet of small luggers. The whole fleet was, it is said, lost in a storm overnight, some time towards the end of the nineteenth century (though much earlier dates have also been suggested), and fishing immediately died, although no evidence of this fact survives. Today it is a deserted village owned by the National Trust. Port Isaac, on the other hand, thrives from tourism, having had a pilchard fishery before the sixteenth century and a pier built sometime around then. In 1850 there were forty-nine fishing boats registered and two boat building yards, the last of which, run by Harry Hills, closed in the 1960s. Fishing today consists mostly of potting, and fresh seafood is landed on The Platt almost daily.

Port Gaverne, around the corner, exported Delabole slate, and was home to a thriving shipbuilding industry. Romantic Boscastle, further north, with its spectacularly tricky entrance from the sea, had a pier erected in the sixteenth century and another when this first one was washed away. It is not a very safe harbour though it did export ore from nearby mines. Bude, on the border with Devon, developed through the export of agricultural goods, with a canal being built in the nineteenth century. Fishing never figured in either place to any extent.

North Cornish boats were generally registered in St Ives (SS) or Padstow (PW).

An old postcard of the harbour at Newquay with trading vessels and a couple of gigs.

Newquay with many boats from St Ives and other East Cornish ports, up for the herring season.

Luggers leaving the harbour. The men, women and children on the quay appear to be Victorian holidaymakers, judging by the clothes they are wearing. This is probably in the late summer when many boats from other ports of Cornwall came for the season.

A posed picture aboard what appears to be a new transom-sterned boat, on the beach at Newquay.

Newquay Harbour in the summer. The four boats drawn up under the cliffs are luggers whilst many of the smaller boats on the right and foreground are crabbers. A steam gentleman's yacht sits upon the beach alongside another private yacht. This is probably in the height of summer, before the herring season.

The Newquay motorised boat registered as PW89 afloat in the harbour. This photograph was probably taken some time around the Second World War. She has a fair amount of sheer on the deck and it has been suggested that this boat was in fact Scottish-built.

Newquay Harbour in 2008.

Padstow Harbour with several gaff-rigged boats. Though they are registered there is no sign of any fishing gear.

Two larger boats, one a smack and the other a ketch, in Padstow in what now is a floating harbour. These are most likely trading vessels, as Padstow's primary function as a port was to serve the wider countryside.

Padstow was a popular port for steam drifters from the east coast of England, come for the herring season in the 1920s. These are all either Lowestoft (LT) or Great Yarmouth (YH) registered vessels. Many of these boats were steam trawlers/drifters, in that they trawled the Irish Sea and Irish coast and then converted to drifting for the herring season.

Steam trawlers from Lowestoft at Padstow. Because of Padstow's connection to the national rail network in 1899 it became a popular landing port because fish could now be rushed to Billingsgate, in the capital, in several hours.

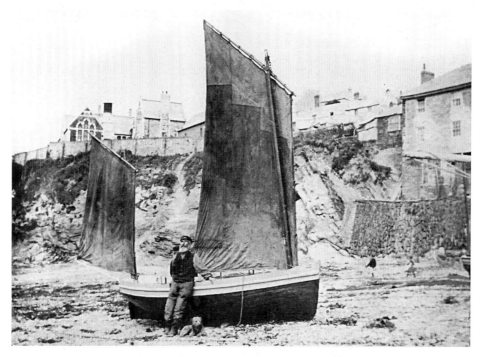

The Port Isaac lugger *Mizpah* with its owner Capt. George Bennett standing alongside, *c.*1895. This boat was typical of the small beach boats that worked from these three 'ports' up to the Second World War. These worked crab pots in summer as well as hand lining and long-lining. In autumn and winter they drift-netted for pilchards and herring.

Martin Castle, George Bennett's great-great-grandson, alongside his replica Port Isaac boat *Rebecca Kate*, built in 2001, which has a slightly different rig and a steel centreplate.

The beach at Port Isaac with a haul of pilchards being unloaded in about 1905.

7

PILCHARD FISHING

The frantic work of pilchard seining involved a whole team of men, seen here emptying the pilchards from the seine net into tuck baskets.

LOADING A CART WITH FISH TO BE CONVEYED TO THE SALTING CELLARS

WHEN THE CIRCLE OF NETS IS COMPLETE THOUSANDS OF

A WATCHER SIGNALLING TO THE MEN IN BOATS THE EXACT SPOT WHERE
TO DROP THEIR NETS

THE FISHERMEN LIFTING THE FISH FR

THE PILCHARD-FISHING IND

DRAWN

ATTRACTED TO THE SPOT TO FEED OFF THE ENCLOSED FISH

PLACING THE NET INTO POSITION TO SURROUND THE SHOAL

INTO THE BOATS BY MEANS OF BASKETS

A WATCHER ON THE HILL LOOKING OUT FOR A SHOAL OF PILCHARDS

Y AT ST IVE'S, CORNWALL

H, R.I.

Pilchards were once to Cornwall what herrings were to Scotland, or sardines to Portugal. It is said that was a Cornish phenomenon, though this is not strictly true as large amount of pilchards were also fished off the south-west coast of Ireland in the late eighteenth century, and by a small Welsh fishery from Fishguard in the nineteenth.

However, it certainly was the principal Cornish fishery, and predates any other of importance in the county, as confirmed by Richard Carew in his 1602 survey. Indeed, most of today's fishing harbours were based on pilchards, and other quays and clusters of buildings along the coast, apart from those already mentioned, were built to service this fishery. One good example of this is the small harbour of Polkerris, today the haunt of boats visiting the pub, or tourists walking the beach past the old pilchard cellars. This little hamlet was once the most important fishing station along this coast. St Austell Bay, over which Polkerris looks, was once called Polkerris Bay, a reminder of its grandeur in the pilchard world.

The pilchard cellars, or palaces, said to be the biggest in the county, are easily accessible. They were fishing here in 1534, and most probably well before that. The pier was built in the 1730s to protect the fleet, and for a further century and a half fishing dominated the inhabitants lives. You can almost smell it! But by the late nineteenth century the pilchards deserted this part of the coast and Polkerris fell quiet. Today it is one of those quirky paradises where tourism has not impacted too much on the surroundings, though the pub car park is often full as folk enjoy a drink while the sun sets over the bay.

North Cornwall had more pilchard seines than the south and considered this the only way to catch the fish, but the East Cornish, Mount's Bay and St Ives fishers set many more miles of drift nets. St Ives itself had more than 280 pilchard companies registered, though only twenty could work at any one time. Laws were passed to ensure that these drifters, or drivers, didn't break up the shoals as they headed up the coast from the Scilly Isles, and they had to fish more than three miles from land. Seines, as we have heard, were company affairs, not in today's corporate sense of the word, but companies of men who combined their efforts and finances to form teams. To do this they needed three boats, two nets, a cellar ashore to cure the fish in and a good group of men, numbering up to twenty, with more employed ashore.

Seining involved the setting of a net around a shoal of pilchards. The massive shoals gave their presence away by colouring the sea from about July onwards. Red, purple and silver stains would be seen from above, and predatory fish would follow whilst flocks of seabirds, especially gannets, dived upon the shoals in vast numbers. To them it was an eating frenzy. Once the shoals appeared the fishers got down to work. The largest boat was the 'stop seiner', a six-oared boat up to 40ft in length, open, low, broad and fast, which carried the net. This was 440 yards long, thirty-three yards deep in the middle and tapered to about 24ft each end. These folk set the net around the shoal, the operation directed by the Master Seiner in the 'lurker' boat – variously called the 'lurcher' or 'larker' – which was some 16–18ft in length. The other boat carried the tuck-net and was called the 'follower', 'folyer', 'follier' or 'volyer', used to lift the fish out of the water. Onshore was the 'huer' or watcher, stationed in his hut on the cliff top, who alerted the fishers to the presence of shoals. He sometimes directed the operation by a system of semaphore signals, appearing like some madman waving of his arms over his head. Once the shoal was captured, the whole net would be towed into shallower water and the business of emptying it and getting the fish ashore to the cellar to be salted, pressed and packed would begin.

Today there has been a slight renaissance for the pilchard fishers with several boats catching out of Newlyn using a ring-net.

A view of a large seine of pilchards at Porthgwarra, near St Levan. The net, laden with pilchards, is towed to shallow water and emptied. Many thousands of fish would be caught in one seine, and the catch could remain fresh in the net for several days whilst anchored to the seabed.

Seine-net boats at Sennen Cove loaded with the haul.

A dog exploring the remains of what is thought to be the last boat to be involved in seine-netting pilchards at Sennen Cove, 2005.

Boats at Sennen Cove. The larger, double-ended boat is a 'follower' boat.

A view of emptying the pilchard net, this time from a seine belonging to St Ives. There were 285 seines registered there in 1870.

Taking pilchards out of the 'stop seiner', the long boat that carried the main net during the operation, at St Ives.

The beach landing just below Pendeen Head on Cornwall's north coast was built for the pilchard fishery. There is a winch house above and curing sheds atop the slipway. Here, in 2008, several boats were still based for seasonal lobstering and crabbing.

A modern-day haul of pilchards aboard the Newlyn registered boat *Prevail*.

A postcard from 1912 showing pilchards being carried in baskets to the curing house at Brazen Island, Polruan.

8

MOTORISATION

Motorised luggers on the beach at St Ives. *Ebenezer*, on the left, ended up rotting at Lelant. Note the transom-sterned boat on the right.

Motorisation did not dramatically affect the Cornish fleets until about 1907, though it would be fair to say they had already been affected to some extent with some luggers having had steam capstans fitted years before, replacing the earlier flywheel capstans. But it was only after 1907 that motors were adopted to propel their boats. In St Ives, for example, the first engined boats were *Gleaner*, SS123, and *Family*, SS61, in 1910. During the First World War many more were motorised through finances advanced from the Motor Loans Committee of the Ministry of Agriculture, Fisheries and Food. Many of these were Kelvin engines from Glasgow, which many in the fishing fleets favoured, and Cornwall had several Kelvin agents. Within less than two decades the transition was complete: in 1923 there was one sail boat left in Fowey and fifty-seven motor boats, of which thirty-one were one-time sailing luggers. The story was the same in the west of Cornwall where, in 1930, there were thirty-four motorboats registered at Penzance and twenty-five at St Ives.

Cornish boats usually had two engines, the main one on the centre-line for reaching the fishing grounds and another smaller unit on the starboard side for working the nets. This was set at an angle to the centre-line so that the shaft passed over the main shaft and protruded out on the port side. The nets were always set and hauled over the starboard side, thus the propeller was kept clear on the port side. Some boats such as *Lindy Lou*, FY382, had three engines, the third driving a winch to haul in the long-lines. Engines were usually situated forward so that the accommodation could be retained at the after end, unlike most of the Scottish boats that either had the accommodation at the forward, uncomfortable, end or amidships. They were famed for having a long shaft running almost two-thirds of the length of the boat.

Perseverance, CN152, was a ring-net herring boat from Campbeltown that was sold to Cornwall in 1949 and, registered as PZ1, worked out of Porthleven for several years. Although her Kelvin J4 diesel engine was, by the standards of the day, modern, this was soon moved from its position at the aft end of the boat to the forward end, in the Cornish style. It was not until the boat was restored in the late 1970s that it was moved back again to where it had originally been positioned.

Jumbo-ising, as we have already seen, meant lengthening boats by cutting them in half and adding a middle portion. This was common practice amongst boat builders. Indeed, the Scillonian boat builders lengthened many of their pilot cutters when larger cutters were needed. Jumbo-ising occurred even after boats had been fitted with engines, or sometimes when an engine unit was being fitted for the first time.

Opposite above: Some boats even had three engines driving three propellers, this example being St Ives registered *Gratitude*.

Opposite below: Postcard of St Ives: *Francis Stevens*, SS49, with her rig. Many luggers retained their rig because of the unreliability of the early engines that often broke down. She has also adopted legs.

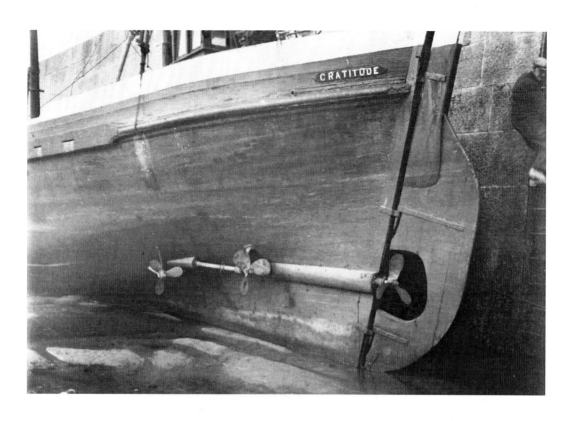

Perseverance, SS40, a motorised mackerel lugger, in St Ives in about 1930. As mentioned in Chapter Two, she was built in St Ives in 1885 and part owned by the local MP and Penzance Mayor C.C. Ross. She worked the spring mackerel and probably sailed to the Irish herring season. During the First World War she was fitted with a Kelvin 26hp engine. The line hauler seen on her deck was powered by steam from the capstan boiler. She was eventually sold in 1945 and renamed *Moss Rose*.

A postcard of a motorboat leaving Newlyn Harbour in the 1950s. By this time most boats had done away with sails as engines became more reliable.

Nazarene, SS114, was built by Bawden of Porthleven, first registered in 1900 and lengthened by Henry Trevorrow of St Ives in 1920. She was regarded as a successful boat. In 1957, on her way to unload 120 stone of pilchards in Newlyn, she ran aground at Pednevounder, near Porthcurno. The crew remained aboard until the tide ebbed, at which time their nets, catch and gear were removed from the boat. On the next high tide, hours after this photo was taken, the boat was smashed to pieces on the rocks. Only her engines remained though most of the gear was later moved up the cliffs by Breeches Buoy.

St Ives boats laid up at Lelant: SS99, *Humility*, sold to Mumbles, 1945; SS634, *Barnabas*, later restored; SS89, steamboat *Gleaner*; SS154, *Reaper*, ex-PZ327; 107SS, *Miriam*, Jumbo.

Snowdrop, FY104, at Mevagissey in August 1965, with pilchard nets aboard.

Erin, FY127, at Mevagissey in August 1965, with pilchard nets aboard.

Lindy Lou, FY382, at Mevagissey in August 1965, with pilchard nets aboard.

9

SURVIVING BOATS AND REPLICAS

Ripple, SS19, believed to have been built in Newlyn in 1896. At 34ft, she was lengthened by 10ft in 1925. She was renowned as one of the most successful pilchard boats in the Newlyn fleet. After leaving fishing she was converted to a gentleman's motor yacht at Looe, and later became a houseboat on the Helford River.

There are somewhere in the region of thirty Cornish luggers still sailing, and at least three replicas. Most were built as sailing luggers and a handful as motor luggers. On top of these several Polperro gaffers still exist, as do a handful of Falmouth Working Boats, a few toshers, half a dozen sailing crabbers and more motorised wooden crabbers as well as many smaller replica boats. A whole host of memories from the beginning and middle of the twentieth century. Some of these boats are shown here.

Ripple was eventually bought by John Lambourne of Newlyn where he and a team of shipwrights rebuilt her. She was launched once again in 2007 and is seen here in Falmouth awaiting her rig.

Barnabas, SS634, was built in 1881 by Henry Trevorrow above Porthgwidden Beach, St Ives. She was one of the smallest mackerel drivers and kept fishing until 1954 after which she was converted to a yacht and kept in Falmouth. She was taken over by the maritime trust in the late 1960s and restored in the 1980s. She returned to St Ives in her centenary year and when the Cornish maritime trust was formed in 1994, about the time this photo was taken, she became their flagship.

She has recently been re-launched after a considerable rebuild, partly financed by the Heritage Lottery Fund, and is seen here entering Mousehole Harbour in 2008.

Pioneer, PZ277, was built by William Paynter in St Ives in 1899 for the Hendy family. She was 35ft in length and was built with a steam engine and worked as a drifter. Earlier in the twentieth century she was lengthened to her present 47ft. She fished using all manner of methods, latterly trawling. The steam engine was removed in 1947 and replaced with a Kelvin until, five years later, this was replaced with a Lister Blackstone JP3. The Hendys finally sold her to Cyril Gascoigne in 1966, and he used her for diving and salvage operations. By 1991 she was in a derelict state in Newlyn Harbour.

Pioneer was bought by Jim Richards and taken to Hayle where he undertook a complete restoration. She is being launched once again in 1999. Here she is seen sailing across St Ives Bay in 2007.

The 44ft lugger *Snowdrop*, FY104, was built in Porthleven in 1925 with an engine fitted, though she still retained a shortened rig. She fished out of Mevagissey until the late 1970s after which she passed into private hands. Today she has been re-rigged and is seen here sailing in Douarnenez Bay in 2008.

Children's Friend, PZ101, is a Scottish seine-netter converted and rigged as a Mount's Bay lugger by Billy Stevenson.

Opposite below: Rosalind, ex-*Susan*, SS185, built in St Ives in 1885, is now in the USA. This boat, along with *Barnabas* and *Ripple*, are the only double-ended Mount's Bay boats to survive.

Luggers *Ocean Pride*, PZ134, and *Children's Friend* off Mousehole in 2006. *Ocean Pride* was built by Henry Peake of Newlyn in 1919 as the last boat built on Tolcarne Beach. She was ordered by two brothers who fell out during the building process so that she ended up, at 42ft, shorter than planned, as one brother withdrew from the partnership. She worked out of Mousehole and was only one of two counter-sterned boats there. She was converted for pleasure after leaving fishing in 1991.

The small 28ft lugger *Joyance* under restoration in about 1997.

Above: Joyance was built in 1925 by Frazier of Mevagissey. Here she is seen sailing at the Looe Lugger Regatta in 2007.

Right: The Looe lugger *Guide Me*, FY233, built by Peter Ferris in 1911 for W. Pengelly as a pilchard driver. In 1966 she was sold to owners in the Solent and eventually bought by Jono and Judy Brickhill who restored her with an original rig. Having no engine, they sailed her to Brazil. Afterwards they sailed to Cape Town and later back to America before basing themselves at Gweek. She is seen here sailing in Douarnenez Bay in July 2008.

Our Daddy, FY7, built by Dick Pearce of Looe as the last lugger in the town. She was owned by J.E. Pengelly and skippered by his son Alfred John, author of the book *Oh, For A Fisherman's Life*. She fished for sixty-five years before being sold, and today is dandy-rigged and used for charter work out of Looe.

Opposite above: The lugger *Maid Marion* was built in 1925 as the *Westward* by twenty-three-year-old Percy Mitchell in his new yard at Porthmellon. At 39ft it was the biggest boat he had been asked to build and his bandsaw was not man enough to cut the oak which he therefore ordered ready-cut from Lang & Co of Liskeard. In 1935 she was sold to Porthleven, where she was renamed after the new owner's daughter. In the Second World War she sailed for Dunkirk but was diverted to Le Havre where she brought home a boatload of soldiers. Owned by David Hunt and kept in the River Deben, seen here in 2005 on her mooring, she is now a member of the Dunkirk Little Ships Association.

Opposite below: The lugger *Erin*, FY127, was built by Frazier of Mevagissey in 1904 as *Ibis* for the Lakeman family, and later taken to France for many years until returning to Cornwall in 2002. Today, painted Looe yellow, she is owned by Paul Greenwood who has done more than anyone else to revitalise interest in these Cornish luggers by establishing the biennial Looe Lugger Regatta.

The Polperro gaffer *Vilona May*, FY20, at Looe in 2007. Built in Looe in 1896, she is rumoured to have sailed to Australia in the 1950s though there seems to be no evidence to support the theory. She has sailed across the Atlantic, up to Boston and as far north as Greenland before returning home to Cornwall.

The lugger *Veracity* is a replica of a Mount's Bay pilchard driver of the same name, registered as PZ111 and originally built by J. Blewett of Newlyn for P. Humphries of Mousehole. She is fully decked with raised fish room hatches, steamed frames and external ballast that gives increased living accommodation and a good speed. She is being followed by the east coast of Scotland boat *Ocean Pearl*, recently restored in Chichester Harbour.

Opposite above: The small lugger *Upwood*, one of two similar boats built by students at the Falmouth Marine School and based on the lines of a Mount's Bay pilchard driver *Veracity*, though scaled down to 22ft from the original 32ft.

Opposite below: Silver Stream, a replica of a Sennen Cove crabber, built by the Falmouth Marine School students from lines taken from the boat of the same name, which was built in 1892.

Opposite above: Internal view of *Silver Harvest*, sister boat to *Silver Stream*.

Opposite below: The small Mevagissey tosher *Little Gem*, built in 1906 by Frazier of Mevagissey. At 18ft she is small for a tosher, built for the Lakeman family who netted and lined with the boat. She is seen here being repainted in 2006.

Gipsy Mermaid was built as the *Robert Barge*, TH12, in 1964 by Curtis & Pape of Looe, builders of many fishing boats after they established a boatyard in Looe. Built as a beam trawler, *Robert Barge* worked out of Plymouth and was regarded as an extremely successful boat, developing various refinements specifically for trawling. Her licence was sold in 1990 and she lay derelict for eight years after which time she was bought by Fred Saunders who spent many years restoring her. She is seen sailing here in 2006.

Little Gem again, motoring out of Mousehole Harbour in 2006.

Silvery Light, built by William Robert Williams on the beach at St Ives in 1884 as a herring drifter, is seen here in Eyemouth in 2003. She first worked out of Great Yarmouth before being sold to Norway under her new name, *Raust*, where she trawled mostly for cod. By 1922 she was coastal freighting and she had an engine fitted in 1931 and the counter-stern added in 1949. By 1988 she had been abandoned and was brought back to England by a new owner who restored her. She spent six years in the Azores before returning to Cornwall, then Eyemouth, and is currently in Amble awaiting further restoration work.

10

FESTIVALS

An assortment of mainly Cornish boats at the Sea, Salts & Sail Festival at Mousehole, 2006.

Thankfully, the Cornish fishing boat aficionados don't go overboard with festivals and regattas. There is the Looe Lugger Regatta one year and the Sea, Salts & Sail at Mousehole the following. There are usually quite a few luggers at each of these events, unless the weather is particularly dire, as it was at Mousehole in 2008. Nevertheless, three hardy boats did turn up.

The Falmouth Working Boats often race at weekends in the summer but, as already mentioned, most of these boats are very different from their working days. This is not to denigrate them, but as a point of interest many are fibreglass and their rigs are not working rigs. The Falmouth Working Boat Association is a haven for keen sailors.

With France 100 miles across the Channel, Cornish boats often appear at French festivals. Breton boats also come over to Cornwall. I remember several years ago being at the Looe Lugger Regatta. The weather was giving us south-westerly gales on the Saturday, and though many boats had turned up, including several Breton craft, it was too windy to race. We ended up playing cricket in the harbour at low water, French, English and Cornish sloshing around in the wet sand and puddles until the waters returned. The next day the boats went racing. In between there was a bit of imbibing and tall stories. It is much the same across the Channel. Nothing is taken too seriously, which suits me! The common factors are an enthusiasm for working boats, keen sailing when the weather is right and a spirit of fun and comradeship, all washed down with plenty of food and drink and chatter about life in general.

Opposite: Dried out boats in Mousehole Harbour, 2006.

Right: Gipsy Mermaid, TH12, leaving the festival at Mousehole in 2006.

Below: L–R: the bows of the Manx nobby *Gladys* and the luggers *Pioneer, Ocean Pride* and *Happy Return.*

Left to right: Stern view of the same: *Happy Return*, *Ocean Pride* and *Pioneer*.

Left to right: *Ibis* and *Snowdrop* at Douarnenez, 2008.

Left to right: *Vilona May* and *Erin* at Douarnenez, 2008.

Guide Me being sailed out of Douarnenez Harbour, 2008.

Sculling the Gorran Haven crabber *Ellen* across
Mousehole's harbour during the festival in 2006.

Pete Goss' replica lugger *Spirit of Mystery*, in which he left Britain in November 2008 to sail to Australia,
mirroring the voyage of the 37ft Newlyn lugger *Mystery* that completed that passage in 1854. *Spirit of Mystery*
was built under the supervision of Chris Rees, co-owner of the Polperro gaffer *Vilona May*. He completed the
voyage in March 2009.

11

FISHING AND DECOMMISSIONING TODAY, AND THE STORY OF A HAPPY RETURN

A typical view overlooking boats at Newlyn. The boat in the foreground is *Excellent*, PZ513.

Today's Cornish fishery, like much of that in the rest of Britain, is a very different story to the days of the Cornish luggers and their counterparts. Most of the pilchard fishery has gone, as have the herring. Newlyn, as we have seen, lands the bulk of the catch, much of which is exported to the Continent. Looe lands the second greatest tonnage, though Padstow, Newquay (recently of Jamie Oliver fame) and Mevagissey still run small fleets, as do other odd coves with their crabbers potting for lobsters and crabs.

It was probably in the 1970s that the greatest change in Cornish fishing came about. Long-lining was declining though the mackerel trade was booming, encouraging boats from all over Europe to join in, including factory ships from Eastern Europe. So much was caught, indeed, that the stocks were almost wiped out. Then, in 1974, the first of the Cornish beam trawlers arrived. Gillnetting for hake encouraged others to veer away from potting and traditional trawling. The Common Fisheries Policy saw Britain's fishing grounds flooded by boats from other countries. In more recent years, after a severe cutting of the fleet, Cornish boats are fishing relatively successfully, though many are far from happy. Turmoil over EU control continues. And though mackerel and herring fishing continues as in other parts of Britain, most is sent to be processed into animal feed. What an utter waste!

However, compared to the rest of Britain, boat building in the south-west is flourishing. Foremost in the building of wooden fishing boats today is C. Toms & Sons of Polruan. Charley Toms took over Hunkin's Yard in 1967, though they had been building boats there long before that. Charley is Alan Toms' grandfather, and Alan runs the yard today. They still build wooden fishing boats, as well as steel boats, and several of these wooden craft have gone up to Scotland over the last decade. They have also built, over the years, dozens for Cornish fishing, including several that joined the Padstow registry.

But they are not alone in building from wood, as timber boat building is enjoying a renaissance. As yet the fishermen of Cornwall aren't persuaded, though who knows what is around the corner. Cockwells of Falmouth are currently building two Bristol Channel pilot cutter replicas,

Excellent was built as *Efficient* in Fraserburgh in 1931, as a herring drifter. In 1937 she moved to Newlyn and was renamed. Here she is fitted out as a trawler.

A good catch aboard the *Excellent* in the mid-1970s.

Excellent in the late 1990s, fitted out for gill-netting in the Western Approaches, seen here sailing for fun. She remains the oldest working fishing boat in the British fleet.

The beam trawler *Cornishman*, PZ512, built in Holland in 1971 and owned by W. Stevenson & Sons in 2005.

The wooden fishing boat *Eilean a Cheo*, BRD7, built by C. Toms & Sons in about 2002 for owners in the Isle of Skye.

Scottish-built fishing boats at Looe in 1998.

after launching their first one in 2007. They have also built wooden motor launches and ferry boats for Falmouth. Down in the Gweek boatyard there are several folk working in wood, Luke Powell of Working Sail being the most prolific as he completes his seventh Scillonian pilot cutter. Given the chance any of these would build fishing boats from wood. John Moor of Mevagissey repairs wooden boats and, if the oppurtunity presented itself, would also build. Oh yes, wooden boat building is very much alive!

DECOMMISSIONING

Decommissioning was the European way of decreasing the number of fishing boats in the European Union fleet by paying the fishermen to leave. Unfortunately it meant that dozens were scrapped and cut up, set alight or pushed into landfill sites. Because many of these boats were older wooden boats, there was a direct loss to Britain's maritime history. Hundreds were destroyed. Several years ago I spent half a day watching one such boat be pulled apart. It was not a pleasant experience as the JCB 'dib–dibbed' into the wooden structure with a front jibber, only managing to pull away scraps of timber at any one time. Each boat took a week to dismantle, the wooden remains were burnt and the steel and everything else taken to landfill sites. This old boat was quite rightly resisting for, even though it was thirty or forty years old, the timber was strong and the boat as seaworthy as the day it was launched. That is what makes this government policy so daft: to be breaking up perfectly good boats. There are other ways of ensuring one particular boat doesn't fish again. No one has ever been able to fully explain to me why, when it was the fishing licence that governed what fish a boat could catch, and this licence was surrendered on

Four views of the boat *Tudor Rose III* being
demolished by a JCB at Newlyn in 1998.

decommissioning, it mattered if that particular boat did fish again. The fisherman would, after all, have to buy a new licence from another fisherman. At the time we described the policy as 'legalised vandalism', a description that certainly got under the skin of government ministers. Sadly the process continues today, though most of these boats are steel. All the wooden ones have been destroyed.

HAPPY RETURN, FE5

Folkestone had some 600 fishermen aboard 110 fishing boats at the turn of the twentieth century, and the majority of these craft were Cornish-built. One such double-ended lugger was *Good Intent*, FE21, owned by Jack Saunders. However, this lugger was wrecked in a particularly violent storm in October 1904, though the crew were saved by the lifeboat. A boat to replace

Above: Happy Return on the beach of Folkestone Harbour soon after her arrival there.

Opposite above: Because of intervention by, amongst others, the newly formed 40+ Fishing Boat Association, in 1995 several vessels were allowed to escape chopping up if they were taken ashore. Here the *Confide*, PZ741, is seen at Land's End as a static display.

Opposite below: A couple of years later, after more lobbying of the government, a few boats were allowed to remain at sea as long as guarantees were given that they didn't ever fish again. *Lindy Lou*, FY382, was one of these, and she is seen here in Falmouth a couple of years after she ceased fishing. Built by Curtis & Pape, Looe, in 1947, as a pilchard driver, one of two similar craft, she was bought by the Blamey family of Mevagissey in 1955. They drifted for pilchards, hand-lined for mackerel and long-lined and later wreck-netted. John Moor, who had built several wreck netters, re-engined *Lindy Lou* in 1971. Before she was decommissioned in 1998 she was one of the most successful boats in Mevagissey. She is still based in Falmouth where she is owned by local photographer Andy Campbell.

A postcard view of Folkestone in the early 1950s with *Happy Return* in the foreground. By this time she had had a wheelhouse added and her rig had been removed though the masts were retained to act as hoists.

Happy Return back in Cornwall sailing in the Sea, Salts & Sail regatta at Mousehole in 2006.

Good Intent was the Kitto-built *Happy Return*, costing £150 and funded by public subscription. She arrived in Folkestone in time for the start of the 1905 fishing season, registered as FE5, and a few years later had a Kelvin 7hp petrol/paraffin engine installed. For over thirty years *Happy Return* worked drift nets and trawls from the port. Just prior to 1939 she was sold to Johnny Fagg and laid up throughout most of the war, to be sold again in 1946 to William Grayling and worked until being laid up again in 1958, before being sold once more in 1961 to William Gale. She worked for seven more years from Folkestone before being sold to Kings Lynn where she was renamed *Britannia* and registered as LN224. She worked the cockle beds of the Wash until being bought by Peter Barrett of Swanage. In 1998 she was decommissioned and threatened with being scrapped. However, due to lobbying by the 40+ Fishing Boat Association members and others, the *Britannia* passed into the ownership of the National Fishing Heritage Centre in Grimsby, from where she was leased to the Mount's Bay Lugger Association to replace their earlier boat, *Orion*, which they had discovered to be Scottish and not Cornish built as they had at first believed! The MBLA changed the boat's name back to the *Happy Return* and have since rebuilt her back to her original 1904 state and, based in Penzance, sail her each year to a variety of Cornish and Breton ports and festivals.

THE NEWLYN AND ST IVES SCHOOL OF ARTISTS

No work on Cornish fishing craft can be complete without a brief mention of the artists that came to Newlyn and St Ives in the late nineteenth century. Already we have seen that William Daniell passed through during his tour of Britain in the 1820s, and though he came as an ethnographer he was by no means the first artist to visit and make illustrations or paintings of the area. Joseph Mallord Turner had already made two visits to Cornwall a decade earlier, even though Cornwall was remote and distant from the rest of Britain until 1859 when the railway over the River Tamar opened up the county to visitors.

However, it was not until the late 1870s that a trickle of artists began arriving in Newlyn on extended visits, many of which had trained or worked in France and had painted Breton ports. Newlyn was at the time a poor and miserable place, but the natural beauty, the light and the work of fishing readily attracted these people. The earliest artist to take up residence in the village was J. Henry Martin in 1873, and others soon followed. Walter Langley arrived in 1880 and Edwin Harris a year later. By 1882 both these men were in residence. One of the most prominent and longstanding members was Stanhope Forbes, who came in 1884. By the end of that decade there were almost twenty resident artists. Forbes and Langley remained there for the rest of their lives.

Several miles across the peninsula, St Ives began attracting well-known artists after James McNeill Whistler visited over the 1883/'84 winter. Again it was the intense light, the dramatic coastline and constantly changing sea, as well as the Mediterranean feel about the place, that captivated them enough to set up an artists' club there in 1888.

Charles Napier Hemy, one of the most accomplished marine painters of the late nineteenth century, settled in Falmouth in the early 1880s, and even converted a 40ft seine boat into his studio. Although not of the Newlyn or St Ives Schools, he visited Newlyn. As a keen sailor he understood the sea in all its shifting movements, and painted some of the finest pictures of Cornish fishing craft I have ever seen, whilst in his 1885 picture, *Pilchards*, he produced one of the finest and expressive portraits of that fishery.

What these artists have, a century or so later, left us with in these examples of British art are magnificent impressions of a fishing industry beginning to awaken from insular subsistence to the beginnings of a major trade. Sadly, however, as Newlyn's harbour developed, around the turn of the century, many of the artists began leaving. In St Ives, which was always more of a seasonal tourist attraction than Newlyn, the artists remained 'realist', rejecting modernism until well into the twentieth century. However, it was during the closing years of the nineteenth century that the best depictions of fisher folk and fishing craft can be seen. Apart from those mentioned and included here, there were, of course, many others not of the schools that painted Cornish fishing craft over these years. Furthermore, many contemporary painters have followed the same path. Cornish fishing boats, their harbours and beaches, and their fishers, continue to attract and inspire artists from all over. Finally, there are the local artists, such as Roger Lowry.

Percy Robert Craft (1856–1935) *Tucking a School of Pilchards, 1897*. Oil on canvas, 142 x 212cm. (Penlee House Gallery & Museum, Penzance)

AFTERMATH

Subsequent to the initial submission of this book, several other photos worthy of mention appeared.

In my earlier book *The Slopemasts – A History of the Lochfyne Skiffs* I wrote about the Scottish boat *Perseverance* that I owned for several years. *Perseverance* spent a few years fishing out of Porthleven, and photographs 2 and 4 were sent to me following the publication of the aforementioned book.

Photo 1: In April 2009 the seventh Scillonian pilot cutter *Amelie Rose* was launched by Cornish boatbuilder Luke Powell at his yard in Gweek. She is pictured here sailing a few days after her launch.

Photo 3: The lugger *Guiding Star* sailing off Looe in 2007 (see page 42).

'*Moss Rose*, SS40', 2007, by Roger Lowry. See page 29 for photos of this luggger, which was originally named *Perserverance*.

'*Happy Return*, FE5', 2007, by Roger Lowry. See pages 117 and 118 for photos of this luggger, which sails from Penzance today.

'*The Pioneer*, PZ277', 2007, by Roger Lowry. See pages 91 and 92 for photos of this boat.

PHOTOGRAPH CREDITS

t = top, m = middle, b = bottom

Alf Trenear	66t
Billy Stevenson	110, 111b
Bryan Roberts	79t, 79b right
Carol Williams	32t
Cornish Maritime Trust	65b, 90b
Cornwall County Library	80t
C. Toms and Sons	112b
Dellon Boothby	42t
Donald Perkin	30b
Fred Saunders	101t
Jan Pentreath	18t, 18b, 19t, 19b, 20t, 21t, 21m, 21b, 22t, 24t, 26t, 47, 48, 49t, 50t, 50b, 51m, 53m, 54t, 54b, 56m, 56b, 71t, 72t, 73t
Jim Richards	91b, 92t
John Buchanan and Heidi Beman	53t, 100b
John Gale	117, 118t
John Lambourne	89
John McWilliams	27b, 29t, 29b, 43t, 43m, 43b, 44t, 52b, 62t, 62m, 62b, 63t, 71b, 86t, 87b, 88t, 88m, 88b, 125 all
Jonny Nance	64m
Martin Castle	73b, 74t
Martin Ellis	82t
Newquay Old Cornwall Society	69b, 70t, 70m, 70b
Nicky Dixon	92b
Richard Major	28b, 83, 85t
Robert Simper	64b
Roger Hosking	32b
Royal Cornwall Museum	72b
St Ives Museum	30t, 59, 63b right, 64t

The rest have either been taken by the author or belong to his collection.

BIBLIOGRAPHY – A SELECTION

Bartlett, John, *Ships of North Cornwall*, Padstow, 1996

Carew, Richard, *The Survey of Cornwall 1602*, Redruth, 2000

Cross, Tom, *The Shining Sands – Artists in Newlyn and St Ives 1880-1930*, Tiverton, 1994

Davies, Alun, *The History of the Falmouth Working Boats*, Falmouth, 1989

Greenwood, Paul, *Once Aboard A Cornish Lugger*, Clifton-upon-Teme, 2007

Harris, Keith, *Hevva! Cornish Fishing in the Days of Sail*, Redruth, 1983

Hill, H. Oliver, 'East Cornish Luggers' in *The Mariner's Mirror*, vol.21 (3), 1935, pp225-244

Kittridge, Alan, *Cornwall's Maritime Heritage*, Truro, 2003

Mannering, J. (ed.), *The Chatham Directory of Inshore Craft*, London, 1997

March, Edgar J., *Sailing Drifters*, London, 1952

– , *Inshore Craft of Britain in the Days of Sail and Oar*, vol.2, Newton Abbot, 1970

McNab, Sue, *Barnabas – A St Ives Mackerel Driver*, Porthleven, 2007

McWilliams, John, *Maritime St Ives*, St Ives, 2006

– , *Breton Fishermen in Cornwall and Scilly*, St Ives, 2007

Mitchell, Percy, *A Boatbuilder's Story*, Mevagissey, 1968

Nance, R.M., 'West Cornish Fishing Luggers before 1850' in *The Mariners Mirror*, vol.30 (2), 1944, pp93-108

Noall, Cyril, *Cornish Seines and Seiners*, Truro, 1972

Oliver, A.S., *Boats and Boatbuilding in West Cornwall*, Truro, 1971

Pengelly, A.J., *Oh, For A Fisherman's Life*, Falmouth, 1979

Powell, Margaret, *Master of the Sea*, Charles Napier Hemy RA, RWS, Penzance, 2004

Simper, Robert, *The Lugger Coast*, Ramsholt, 2003

Smylie, Mike, *Traditional Fishing Boats of Britain and Ireland*, Shrewsbury, 1999

Sugar-Fenton, M., *The Rosebud and the Newlyn Clearances*, Truro, 2003

White, E.W., *British Fishing-Boats and Coastal Craft*, London, 1950

There are also a whole host of booklets pertaining to individual harbours and beach landings, too numerous to mention though equally informative.

MIKE SMYLIE IS...

A maritime historian concentrating on the fishing industry and fishing and other working vessels. He has written, and continues to write, widely on the subject for various magazines including *Classic Boat*, *The Boatman*, *Watercraft*, *Maritime Heritage* and *Maritime Life and Traditions*, the latter in which he also has written of the fishing craft of India. *Classic Boat* has run numerous articles on both British fishing vessels and those of the European continental waters, as well as various other series. He also occasionally writes for the weekly newspaper *Fishing News* as well as contributing to the European Maritime Heritage newsletter. He is a member of The Society for Nautical Research, The South West Maritime History Society, The Yachting Journalists' Association, The Coble and Keelboat Society and the Anglesey Antiquarians.

Mike Smylie is the author of ten published books: *The Herring Fishers and other Vignettes* (a book of poetry written in 1996), *The Herring Fishers of Wales* (Carreg Gwalch, 1998), *Traditional Fishing Boats of Britain and Ireland* (Waterline, 1999), *Kipperman & the Red Herring* (self-published, 1999), *Anglesey and its Coastal Tradition* (Carreg Gwalch, 2000), *Herring – A History of the Silver Darlings* (Tempus, 2004), *Working the Welsh Coast* (Tempus, 2005), *The Slopemasts – the History of the Lochfyne Skiffs* (The History Press, 2008), *Fishing the European Coast* (The History Press, 2009) and *Working the Irish Coast* (Nonsuch Publishing, 2009). This is his eleventh book.

He is co-founder of the 40+ Fishing Boat Association, founded in 1995 against the background of scrapping of decommissioned fishing vessels. He is editor of their thrice-yearly magazine *Fishing Boats*.

He is also known as 'Kipperman' for his work in promoting the consumption of herring for its healthy benefits, for which he was awarded the BBC Radio 4 Food Campaigner/Educator Award in November 2004. He has appeared on radio – both local and national – numerous times and occasionally on TV.

Trained as a naval architect, he obtained an HND with distinction in 1975 and also became a Technician Engineer (T.Eng). In 2003 he was awarded an MPhil for his research work on the fishing craft of the Clyde at the Scottish Institute of Maritime Studies at St Andrews University. He also has a RYA Yachtmaster Offshore certificate and was also, at one time, a BSAC Sport Diver. His other interests include walking, climbing and mountaineering, ancient fish-traps, sailing and travelling. He has three children; two sons and a daughter, and spends his time between Bristol and a mountain village in Greece, when not on the road.

See more at www.kipperman.co.uk

Other titles available from The History Press:

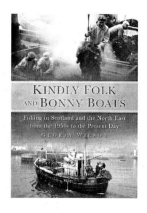

Kindly Folk and Bonny Boats: Fishing in Scotland and the North-East from the 1950s to the Present Day

GLORIA WILSON

This book provides a pictorial appreciation of the boats and fishing communities of Scotland and North-East England from the 1950s to the present, making use of Gloria Wilson's unique collection of photographs. It includes information on boat design and construction as well as some rarely seen naval architects' line plans.

978 0 7524 4907 4

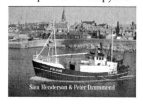

Fishing Boats of Cambeltown Shipyard

SAM HENDERSON AND PETER DRUMMOND

Competition from foreign shipyards moved into a new dimension from the mid-nineties onwards. In addition, decommissioning, restricted days at sea and shrinking quotas have left the Scottish fleet a shadow of its former self. However, by the beginning of the twenty-first century, things were beginning to look up for the remaining vessels, including surviving boats built in Cambeltown Shipyard.

978 0 7524 4765 0

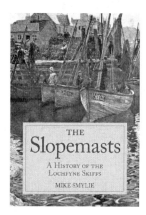

The Slopemasts: A History of the Lochfyne Skiffs

MIKE SMYLIE

The West Coast of Scotland has its own peculiarities that have led to altogether different boats developing through their usage. Amongst these craft is the Lochfyne skiff that emerged from several generations of innovation and which resulted in one of the prettiest workboats to have graced the British shores.

978 0 7524 4774 2

Working the Welsh Coast

MIKE SMYLIE

The people of Wales have always looked to the sea. Given that the country is surrounded on three sides by water, it is not surprising that the sea has played a vital role in the development of the culture and industry of the country. This book looks at the types of vessels used along the coast, for both fishing and coastal trade, including Tenby Luggers, Mumbles Oyster Skiffs, Cleddau Compass-net boats, Aberystwyth beach boats, Aberporth herring boats, Welsh nobbies, coracles and River Dee salmon boats, and Welsh topsail schooners, with inset spreads looking at different sectors of the Welsh maritime industry and heritage.

978 0 7524 3244 1

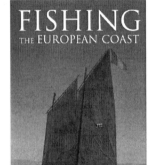

Fishing the European Coast

MIKE SMYLIE

No-one knows when the first fishing boat set out to sea, although river fishing by boat was quite likely the earlier. Mosaics from the Mediterranean show vessels encircling shoals dating from the first century although Egyptian tomb reliefs dated to 6000BC show nets being set. In Britain, we also know that Mesolithic man was moving about by boat, again in about 6000BC. These people, primarily wanderers, were also hunter gatherers. Jesus, we are told, sailed aboard fishing boats on the Sea of Galilee around the early years of the first century AD whilst Caesar noted that wooden boats were in use in Britain sometime after the Roman invasion. Although the roots of some of the vessels may go back many generations, it is really only the last two centuries that concern us. In the main those in these pages are still in existence in some form or other, even if not for their original intended use.

978 0 7524 4628 8

Herring

MIKE SMYLIE

The story of herring is entwined in the history of commercial fishing. For over two millennia, herring has been commercially caught and its importance to the coastal people of Britain cannot be measured. At one point tens of thousands were involved in the catching, processing and sale of herring. They followed the shoals around the coast of Britain and many towns on the East Coast grew rich on the backs of the silver darlings. In addition, for those who have neglected the silver darlings for lesser fish such as cod or haddock, there are numerous recipes to try!

978 0 7524 2988 5

Visit our website and discover thousands of other History Press books.

www.thehistorypress.co.uk